'Call Them to Remembrance'

The Welsh rugby internationals who died in the Great War

Gwyn Prescott

ST DAVID'S PRESS

Cardiff

Published in Wales by St. David's Press, an imprint of
Ashley Drake Publishing Ltd
PO Box 733
Cardiff
CF14 7ZY
www.st-davids-press.com

First Impression – 2014

ISBN 978-1-902719-37-5

British Library Cataloguing-in-Publication Data.
A CIP catalogue for this book is available from the British Library.

*Dedicated to the memory
of all Welsh rugby players who served
in the Great War
1914-1918.*

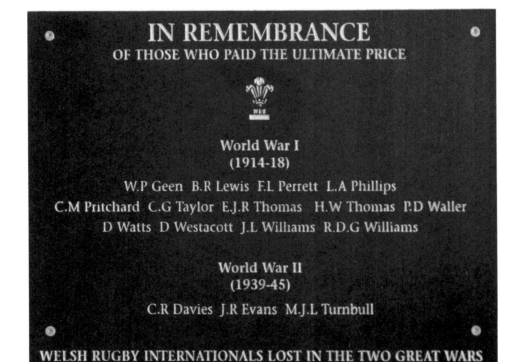

The WRU War Memorial plaque, Millennium Stadium.   [David Dow]

CONTENTS

*A contribution from the royalties generated from the sale of this book
will be donated to the Welsh Rugby Charitable Trust,
which supports those players and their families who
have been severely injured whilst playing rugby football in Wales.*

Further information about the work of the Trust can be found at:

http://www.wrct.org.uk/

FOREWORD

These pages contain an unexplored and untold tale which, from the deepest anguish of the suffering born of their unquestioning bravery, pierces the heart. These were courageous men who in the defence of peace and in seeking to overcome tyranny put their lives at incredible risk and paid the ultimate price. Some have been remembered, some not. This book is a belated acknowledgment of the sacrifice made by 13 Welshmen.

These men are from different parts of Wales. These 13 men had followed different paths in their lives. They were from different walks of Welsh life; a collier as well as a coal exporter, steelworkers and lawyers, those of elementary education as well as those who went to Cambridge and Oxford. In other words a microcosm of what it was to live in an integrated Wales. The common factor which attached to them all is the fact that they played rugby for Wales. Among the millions who died, this honour is what separates these men and why the story is recorded here.

At the core is the solemn contrast between the joy and fun of the game in which each of these men had made their distinctive mark and that of the weariness of spirit that must have overwhelmed them and of the deadly outcome that lay ahead. Of the families, so proud of them, they left behind and of the separation from their homes and friends to suffer unimaginable pain in a foreign field. In the trenches, they must have longed for home and of the thought that one day they would return to feel the free wind in their hair, the smell of freshly-cut hay and the bird song in the distance and once more, who knows, to the wonder of wearing the scarlet jersey of Wales.

As each story unfolds, this mood vibrates through each paragraph and the melancholy that resides between the hope for a glad future and that of the wretched heartache they endured, reverberates through to the next chapter and onto the closing pages.

Theirs was a sacrifice which needs to be told.

Gwyn Prescott with meticulous and sympathetic attention to detail tells the story. We must value his extensive efforts and treasure the record which he provides of these men's lives and which he recovers when they might so easily be in danger of vanishing altogether. This narrative is an essential record.

Gerald Davies

ACKNOWLEDGEMENTS

As with any book of this nature, it could not have been written without the generous help of numerous people, though any errors it contains are entirely my responsibility. I must apologise in advance, if I have inadvertently omitted to acknowledge anyone's assistance.Furthermore, whilst every reasonable effort has been made to obtain copyright clearance for all of the images used in this book, I would be delighted to hear from the small number we have been unable to identify.

Special thanks are due to my many friends in the South Wales Branch of The Western Front Association, in particular Dr. John Dixon for his advice on the military content; Terry Powell for producing the excellent maps while coping with my frequent revisions; Gary Williams for generously providing his superb photographs; and Phil Davies, Angus Evans, Harold Evans, Pat Evans and David Hughes, who also contributed in a variety of ways.

I am especially grateful to Dave Dow (Swansea RFC and Dragon Tales Photography) for his invaluable help with many of the images. Dave is currently assisting the WRU in recording some of their archive materials and I have been fortunate enough to work with him on this. I am also greatly indebted to Steve Rogers (The War Graves Photographic Project); Frederick Sohier (britishcemeteries.webs.com); Pierre Vandervelden, Chris Cosgrove and Jean Cosgrove (inmemories.com); Dick Williams (Gloucester RFC); and Steve Lewis for providing photographs. I would also particularly like to thank Peter Owens (WRU); as well as Katrina Coopey, Tony Davidson, Peter Evans, Bryn Jones and all the staff in Cardiff Library; and Clare Anning, Sarah Lee and, previously, Matthew Christmas of Monmouth School.

There are many others who deserve mention. For help of various kinds, I am indebted to: Diana Chardin, Jeff Childs, Jacqueline Cox, Peter Crocker, Richard Daglish, Mike Dams, Robin Darwall-Smith, Hubert Harries Davies, Joe Devereux, Howard Evans, Huw Evans, Martin Everett, Barry Fleming, Amanda Gillard, Martyn Ham, Andrew Hambling, Frédéric Humbert, John Jenkins, Bernard Lewis, John Lyons, Brian Martin, Richard May-Hill, Peter Monteith, Keith Moore, Gareth Morgan, Nigel Nichols, Colin O'Neill, Sam Parker, Ron Perrett, Jonathon Poyner, Mike Price, Phil Richards, Alan Roberts, Jed Smith, Ceri Stennett, Dennis Thomas, Gareth Thomas, Professor Gareth Williams, Kate Wills and Martin Wills.

I am grateful to my publisher, Ashley Drake, who has enthusiastically supported this project from the outset and has guided me with patience throughout.

I would also like to give my special thanks to Gerald Davies for kindly providing his moving Foreword to this book.

Finally, this book would not have been completed without the continual encouragement and support of the members of my family. I must particularly thank my daughters: Sarah, for her practical help with regard to the production of the book; Anna, for searching out images; and Siân, for taking many of the photographs from around Wales. And of course I also thank my wife, Catherine, for her invaluable help and advice at all times.

INTRODUCTION

Football memories are short. Players whose names should be written in letters of gold in the annals of football are forgotten or half-forgotten: it is a pious duty to call them to remembrance.

W J Townsend Collins, *Rugby Recollections* (1948).

Rugby did not take long to respond to the catastrophic news that war had broken out between Britain and Germany on 4 August 1914. Only three weeks later, the Welsh Rugby Union issued a circular to clubs calling on all players to answer "the urgent call of their King and Country" and there was an immediate response. With players across the country enlisting and clubs like Cardiff announcing they had cancelled fixtures, on 4 September 1914, the WRU went much further than their earlier position. This time the Union now officially suspended all fixtures for the duration of the war and strongly recommended that clubs should give up their grounds for use by the army. Again, they urged "upon all men eligible for service, and particularly footballers, the very great importance of at once

Spectators at a military match at Brighton 31 October 1914. "England" beat "Wales" 24-0.

placing their services at the disposal of the Military Authorities". Of course, rugby continued to be played throughout the war by military teams and, in November 1914, the WRU even agreed to allow other matches, provided they were arranged for charitable or recruiting purposes, but rugby as it had been organised for the previous forty years ceased. Throughout Britain, this remained the position until shortly after the Armistice in November 1918, when clubs were at last permitted to play again.

No reliable records exist of the total number of Welsh rugby players or even internationals who answered the WRU's call. But it is known that thirteen Welsh international players who did, paid the ultimate sacrifice. It is a remarkable characteristic of Britain's participation in the First World War that, for the first seventeen months of that dreadful conflict, the country was able to rely entirely on volunteers to supply its armed forces. Conscription was not introduced until January 1916 and before then – well before in most cases – all thirteen who are the subject of this book had volunteered for active service. Moreover, by that date, three had already sacrificed their lives for King and Country. The reasons why men enlisted were many and complex, but the belief that Britain was fighting a just war was a widely held one.

One of the glories of Welsh rugby is that, from its very early days, it has always enjoyed a broad following from across social and class boundaries. Whereas the English, Scottish and Irish international players who died in the war were predominantly middle or upper class, the thirteen Welshmen reflect the much more socially varied nature of rugby in Wales. Working-class players, as well as those from the professional and commercial middle class and even the landed gentry are all represented. Amongst the thirteen will be found a collier, a docker, a policeman, a steelworker, an engineer, a wholesaler, a coal exporter, a shipping agent, an architect, lawyers, a Royal Navy officer, and a Regular Army officer. Some were educated at elementary school, others at grammar or public school, while four studied at Oxford or Cambridge.

They include players from mid and north Wales as well as the south. One, like many other Welsh internationals of this era, had been born in England. Their clubs at the time they were capped included Cardiff, London Welsh, Maesteg, Mountain Ash, Neath, Newport, Swansea, Blackheath, Cambridge University and Oxford University; while at other periods in their careers, they also played for Aberaman, Aberavon, Brecon, Bridgend, Briton Ferry, Ferndale, Maesteg Quins, Merthyr, Penygraig, Pontardawe, Rhymney and Whitchurch, amongst others.

The story of the thirteen is also largely that of Welsh rugby, from its earliest days up to the First World War. For this reason, the narrative presented here follows the chronological order in which each appeared for Wales. Inevitably there are some gaps, particularly in the 1890s, but their collective careers cover much of this formative period in the history of the Welsh game.

Few of the thirteen are very well known today. Only two made it into Wayne Thomas's list of the hundred best Welsh players in his *A Century of Welsh Rugby Players 1880-1980*. In the words of one of the finest commentators on Welsh rugby, WJ Townsend Collins, "their names were once written in the lists of players, but their deeds were traced in sand, and the wind of oblivion has blown over them." This book is therefore an attempt to recover the memory of these multi-talented and courageous Welshmen, heroes of the rugby field who also gave their lives in the service of their country.

Amongst their stories are those of the Cambridge choral scholar who moved in the same circles as Rupert Brooke and who gave up his job in India to volunteer for the Army; the flying Cardiff winger who impressed Lloyd George; the leading amateur golfer in Wales who represented Newport at five sports, and refused a commission; and the "lion-hearted" hero of the famous Welsh victory over New Zealand in 1905.

My account of the lives of these men is based upon more than ten years of study and research, although it also draws upon a lifelong interest in both the history of Welsh rugby and the First World War. My sources include a range of histories, reference works, military records, and contemporary newspapers, in particular, the reports of "Forward" of the *Western Mail* and "Old Stager" of the *South Wales Daily News*. EHD Sewell's, *The Rugby Football Internationals' Roll of Honour* (1919) was also a very useful initial reference, as was *Who's Who of Welsh International Rugby Players* (1991) by John Jenkins, Duncan Pierce and Timothy Auty. Many of the other sources used are listed in the Further Reading section. On a point of clarification, before the First World War, "football" was a generic term which applied as much to rugby as association and most Welsh rugby clubs were styled simply "football club". The Welsh Rugby Union did not change its name from the Welsh Football Union until 1935. However, in order to avoid confusion, the modern versions of the names of rugby clubs and the WRU are used throughout.

When previously researching the early history of rugby and reviewing contemporary match reports, team lists and photographs, I began to wonder about what might be lying in wait for so many of these rugby footballers after the outbreak of the Great War. This book is respectfully dedicated to all Welsh rugby players who served in that appalling conflict.

Gwyn Prescott
Cardiff, August 2013

Richard Davies Garnons Williams

Born: Llowes, Radnorshire 15 June 1856.
Killed in action: Loos 27 September 1915.

Teams: Magdalen College School, Oxford; Brecon; Trinity College, Cambridge; Royal Military College Sandhurst; Newport; South Wales.

Wales: 1 cap, 1881.

"Llowes" and "Loos" may sound similar but they couldn't be more different places. One is a tiny village in the Wye Valley overlooking the Black Mountains and set in the delightful countryside around Hay-on-Wye. The other is a former coal-mining town lying in the flat industrial landscape of north-east France. They are linked, however, through the life of Richard Davies Garnons Williams, a member of the first ever Welsh international XV to take the field.

Rugby came rather late to Wales. By the 1850s, it was already taking hold in the rest of the British Isles, but the first properly organised rugby clubs didn't emerge in Wales until the early 1870s. Once established, however, the sport was soon enthusiastically embraced by all classes of south Wales society. Richard Davies Garnons Williams was there at the very birth of Welsh rugby and therefore deserves to be recognised as one of the pioneers of the game in Wales. Known as "Williams" during his early life, Richard later adopted the surname "Garnons-Williams" after he was capped by Wales.

Aged fifty-nine when he was killed in action commanding his battalion at the Battle of Loos, Richard was the oldest of all the 135 rugby internationals who lost their lives in the Great War. He was also one of the oldest Welshmen to die in front-line action. The son of the vicar of Llowes in Radnorshire where he was born in 1856, Richard's father inherited Abercamlais, a Breconshire country house, five years later. Richard's mid Wales origins

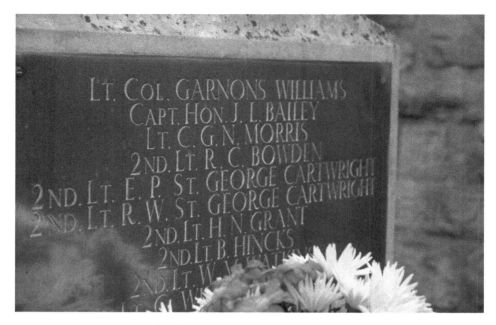

Hay-on-Wye War Memorial.   [Siân Prescott]

may have helped him win selection for Wales, since the organisers of the first ever international team were keen to demonstrate that the Welsh XV (unlike the north dominated soccer XI) was representative of the whole of the country.

Around the time of Richard's birth, rugby was only just emerging from the public schools. There is no evidence to support Guy's Hospital's claim of an 1843 foundation date but it was during the 1850s that the first clubs began to appear. Amongst these were Trinity College Dublin (1854), Liverpool (1857), Edinburgh Academicals (1857) and Blackheath (1858) though, as yet, there were none in Wales. During the 1860s, "clubs" (or more precisely "teams") are known to have existed in Neath, Cowbridge, Cardiff, Newport, Brecon, Abergavenny and Pontypool but these were short-lived. Little is known about their organisation or the rules under which they played. Most appear to have adopted a "hybrid" version of football, involving elements of both rugby and association. By the late 1860s, Llandovery College and probably Lampeter College had taken up the game but the first properly constituted clubs playing rugby did not appear in Wales until the following decade, with the Tredegarville club of Cardiff being amongst the very first in 1870. The big breakthrough, however, came in 1877 with the introduction of the South Wales Challenge Cup, which created immense public interest. From then on Welsh rugby never looked back.

Like many rugby players of this era, Richard enjoyed competing at a variety of sports. At the time of his death, it was even claimed that he had played in goal for Wales in the same year he was capped at rugby. Disappointingly, the Football Association of Wales have no record of such a unique sporting achievement, so perhaps he had taken part in a scratch game involving military sides. He was a good athlete, though. At Magdalen College School and at Sandhurst, he won various competitions for throwing a cricket ball, while he was the Sandhurst champion in both the hammer and the shot. He also rowed at school and at Cambridge.

Cricket was certainly a life-long passion. Besides playing for his school XI and for the Brecon club, he also represented Breconshire on several occasions. Even though he was still only in his teens, his batting helped the county secure two victories over Glamorgan in 1875. The venue for the second of these encounters was the Arms Park and, within a few months, as will be seen, he was back there again, but this time playing representative rugby. He was also a member of the South Wales Cricket Club, where he would have become acquainted with a number of early rugby stalwarts. He certainly would have played cricket for his college at Cambridge and for various military sides during his army career. Even after he had retired from the Army, he remained an active member of Hay-on-Wye CC, captaining them during 1909 when he was in his fifties. His evident love of cricket may have even led to his winning his Welsh cap. During the summer of 1880, when home on leave from the Army, he had a few games of cricket for Newport. These included matches against Chepstow and Monmouth, when he was bowled out by the same man, Edward Peake, who only six months later would be playing *with* him in the Welsh XV: such sporting connections were very common then. There can be little doubt that, when taking part in these games, he came to the attention of Richard Mullock, the secretary of the Newport Cricket and Football Club. Mullock had a far-reaching influence on early Welsh rugby. Under his leadership, Newport dominated the early years of the club game in Wales and he was the driving force behind establishing rugby as the major sport in the Victorian town. He later turned his attention to a much wider audience. Almost single-handedly, and in the face of hostility and condescension from some RFU officials, he managed to arrange the first ever Welsh international match with England in February 1881. Shortly afterwards, Mullock was instrumental in setting up the Welsh Football Union, as the WRU was then known, and he was unanimously elected the Union's first secretary.

At the time RDG Williams was playing, not only was rugby in Wales very much in its infancy, but so too was newspaper coverage of the sport. Consequently, tracing the details of his career is not easy, especially given

Richard Mullock (1851-1920).

his surname. Inevitably, therefore, there has to be some speculation about his playing record. He was introduced to rugby while at public school in Oxford and, since he played cricket for Brecon, he probably also helped out the town rugby club when on vacation. Whilst his team affiliation in some international records is given as Cambridge University, he did not win a Blue there. Though he probably played for Trinity College, he may never have represented the university. He had left Cambridge nearly six years before he was capped, so the references to his being a Varsity player around the time of the international are very misleading. Some early sources show his "club" as Abercamlais. Five miles west of Brecon on the Sennybridge road, it is simply the name of his family home. Though it is confusing to us today, early Welsh teams were often published listing some players by their clubs and others by their place of residence. Demonstrating a poor grasp of geography, WRU handbooks of the 1930s even gave Richard's affiliation as "North Wales". However, the correct entry should read Newport as that is the club he was playing for, albeit briefly, when he was capped at forward by Wales.

He did not spend much time at Cambridge. He went up to Trinity in the autumn of 1874 but left after completing only one academic year in the summer of 1875. At this time, leaving the university without taking a degree was not especially unusual. While at Cambridge, Richard served as a private in the Trinity College Company of the University Rifle Volunteers, a forerunner of the Officer Training Corps. Perhaps this is an indication that all along he was set on pursuing a military career and it may never have been his intention to stay at Cambridge for the full three years.

After leaving Trinity, he spent the remaining months of 1875 at Abercamlais. He kept up his active interest in rugby while there and, in the September, was elected to the first committee of the newly formed South Wales Football Club. Though he missed their historic inaugural fixture at Hereford, he played at forward for South Wales against Clifton in their very next game, held in January 1876 at the Arms Park. Anticipating the hold which rugby was soon to have on the Welsh public, this first ever representative match played in Wales aroused considerable interest and was attended by several hundred highly appreciative spectators. In the heavy conditions, Clifton combined well and defeated South Wales by two goals and three tries to nil. Nevertheless, with the local game growing steadily in popularity, within a year, South Wales were able to gain revenge over Clifton by two tries to nil. However, by then, Richard was no longer available because, in February 1876, he entered the Royal Military College Sandhurst and was

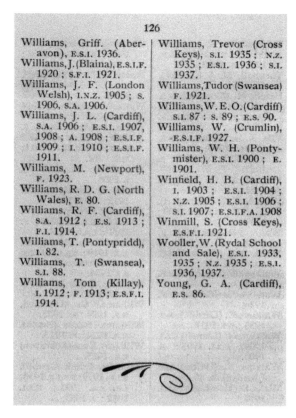

126

Williams, Griff. (Aberavon), E.S.I. 1936.
Williams, J. (Blaina), E.S.I.F. 1920 ; S.F.I. 1921.
Williams, J. F. (London Welsh), I.N.Z. 1905 ; S. 1906, S.A. 1906.
Williams, J. L. (Cardiff), S.A. 1906 ; E.S.I. 1907, 1908 ; A. 1908 ; E.S.I.F. 1909 ; I. 1910 ; E.S.I.F. 1911.
Williams, M. (Newport), F. 1923.
Williams, R. D. G. (North Wales), E. 80.
Williams, R. F. (Cardiff), S.A. 1912 ; E.S. 1913 ; F.I. 1914.
Williams, T. (Pontypridd), I. 82.
Williams, T. (Swansea), S.I. 88.
Williams, Tom (Killay), I. 1912 ; F. 1913 ; E.S.F.I. 1914.

Williams, Trevor (Cross Keys), S.I. 1935 ; N.Z. 1935 ; E.S.I. 1936 ; S.I. 1937.
Williams, Tudor (Swansea) F. 1921.
Williams, W. E. O. (Cardiff), S.I. 87 : S. 89 ; E.S. 90.
Williams, W. (Crumlin), -E.S.I.F. 1927.
Williams, W. H. (Pontymister), E.S.I. 1900 ; E. 1901.
Winfield, H. B. (Cardiff), I. 1903 ; E.S.I. 1904 ; N.Z. 1905 ; E.S.I. 1906 ; S.I. 1907; E.S.I.F.A. 1908
Winmill, S. (Cross Keys), E.S.F.I. 1921.
Wooller, W. (Rydal School and Sale), E.S.I. 1933, 1935 ; N.Z. 1935 ; E.S.I. 1936, 1937.
Young, G. A. (Cardiff), F.S. 86.

WRU handbook 1937-8, showing RDG Williams as from "North Wales". Note the year is also incorrect.

commissioned sub-lieutenant. He was nineteen years old.

Sandhurst had a decent fixture list at that time, so Richard would have been able to test himself against some of the leading London players. In November 1876, he took part in Sandhurst's annual derby with the engineers of the Royal Military Academy Woolwich at Kennington Oval. This ended in a no-score draw and the match must have disappointed the "large and enthusiastic company" as it was "entirely destitute of good play" in the opinion of *The Times*. Completing his officer training shortly afterwards, he was posted to the 38th Regiment and in 1877 transferred to the 7th Regiment (later renamed The Royal Fusiliers), stationed in the London area. He no doubt continued to play, when he could, for military teams or London clubs.

The close relationship between cricket and rugby at Newport has already been noted. It was not therefore surprising that, when Richard began playing occasional games of cricket there while on leave from his regimental depot at Hounslow, he was eventually invited to appear for the club at what was then almost invariably referred to as football. He played in at least three of Newport's fourteen fixtures in 1880-1 and was selected for at least one other. These were some of the club's toughest fixtures that year, and one in particular was a crucial cup semi-final against Cardiff. Matches between these two great rivals have never been for the faint-hearted and this acrimonious clash was certainly no exception. Cardiff had never beaten Newport before and pre-match the *Western Mail* correctly predicted that whoever won this tie would take the cup. Post-match it reported: "The game of rugby has always been quite the rage at Newport ... the excitement on the ground

Wales v England 1881. Back: WD Phillips, G Harding, R Mullock, F Purdon, G Darbishire, E Treharne, RDG Williams. Middle: TA Rees, E Peake, J Bevan, B Girling, B Mann; Front: L Watkins, C Newman, EJ Lewis, R Summers.

was intense throughout." There was fighting on the field and, after Cardiff eventually won by a disputed score, some of the spectators demonstrated their displeasure at the result in a violent way. They surrounded the pavilion and attacked some of the players as they left and even tried to throw the try scorer into the river! It seems, though, that Richard Mullock had been impressed by the commitment shown in the match because he eventually based his team to play England around a core of four Cardiff and six Newport players. Selected in a nine-man pack, RDG Williams was one of the Newport contingent.[1] Over the Christmas holidays he also played for the South Wales XV so, despite being based in London, he was no stranger to many of the leading Welsh players.

Mullock's organisation of this first ever Welsh international team is often criticised and even ridiculed, but much of this criticism is unfair and is based on a somewhat inaccurate but regularly recycled interpretation of the events. It is said that he tried to arrange a trial but it never took place. It did and it was reported in the press. It is widely claimed that players had to be pulled in to the team from the spectators at Blackheath. They were

---

1   Although the Great War was thirty-three years away, the Welsh team also included another career soldier who served in that conflict, Richard Summers.

not: the three replacements were all named reserves. It is also said that the selected players were largely unknown but almost all had previously played for South Wales while the one north Wales representative had played for Lancashire. Whether it was the *strongest* Welsh XV is quite another matter. As it was, the Welsh team's performance was dire and injuries to two players by half-time didn't help. There is no getting away from it, Wales were comprehensively trounced and Mullock later admitted they received a "fearful thrashing". The *Leeds Mercury*'s verdict was that Wales were over-matched from the outset. England scored their first try within five minutes and, throughout the second half, with the wind behind them, they put constant pressure on the Welsh goal-line. The visitors were "altogether puzzled by the scientific play" of their opponents. Even the *Western Mail* had to acknowledge that "the home team were far superior to their opponents in the tactics of passing and were generally much stronger". This all makes uncomfortable reading for Welshmen but at least they can take comfort from the knowledge that within twenty years, when it came to "scientific play" and "the tactics of passing", the rugby boot would be very firmly on the other foot. Just how much stronger England were in 1881 though can be judged by their final tally of thirteen tries, seven conversions and one drop goal. Wales failed to score. Only five of the Welsh team ever wore an international jersey again and Richard Davies Garnons Williams was not one of them.

Thereafter he disappears from the Welsh game. His army career may have now restricted his opportunities to play. In 1884, he was promoted to captain and was stationed in Gibraltar with the 1st Battalion The Royal Fusiliers and then he went on active service with the Fusiliers to Egypt. He married in 1885 and later had two daughters and a son, Roger, who served in The South Wales Borderers during the First World War. From 1887, Richard became Adjutant to the 4th Militia Battalion of his regiment and then he retired from the army in 1892, qualifying as a barrister at the Inner Temple in the same year. He maintained an active involvement in the military, however, and served with the Volunteers as Brigade Major of the South Wales Border Brigade. When he reached fifty in 1906, he resigned his commission, no doubt assuming that his army days were now well and truly over. Having acquired an estate near Hay-on-Wye, he settled into a full and active life of public service in Breconshire, devoting himself to numerous charity, parish and local government responsibilities. Even so, as soon as war was declared, he had no doubt about where his duty now lay. He may have been fifty-eight but he put aside any concerns about this and immediately offered his services to the country again. So in September 1914, he was appointed Major and Honorary Lieutenant Colonel of a local Territorial unit,

Hay-on-Wye Memorial.   *[Siân Prescott]*

the 1st (Brecknockshire) Volunteer Battalion The South Wales Borderers.

In the meantime, his old regiment had begun forming several new "Service" battalions from the many Kitchener recruits who were now pouring in to volunteer at his old barracks at Hounslow. One of these was the 12th Battalion which began collecting there in September 1914 and Major Richard Garnons-Williams was transferred to it as second-in-command. The 12th (Service) Battalion The Royal Fusiliers began preparing for war on the South Downs. Their initial training was blighted by shortages of all kinds, including rifles, equipment, and uniforms and, importantly, experienced officers, so a retired major recalled to active duty would have had a valuable role to play. In June 1915, the 12th Royal Fusiliers moved to Pirbright, Surrey and began their final training, now under the command of the 73rd Brigade, 24th Division.[1]

They landed in France on 1 September 1915. Events then began to move quickly, perhaps too quickly. Instead of receiving any initiation in trench warfare, the 24th Division, together with the equally inexperienced 21st

---

1   Each division in the British Army had three infantry brigades while each brigade was made up of four battalions (reduced to three in 1918).

Division, were allocated to the general reserve for the Battle of Loos. The plan was to launch an attack by six British divisions on the German front line between the La Bassée Canal and Loos; and, once they had created a gap, the reserves would then be sent in to assault the enemy's second line and open up the breakthrough.

The battle commenced on the morning of 25 September. Despite heavy losses, the British made good headway in the south and captured Loos. To the north, progress was slower, but the 9th (Scottish) Division had managed to take the German trenches around the formidable Hohenzollern Redoubt. This was a heavily fortified strongpoint, created by the Germans to defend a pithead known as "Fosse 8" and a slag-heap called "The Dump", both of which gave crucially important views over the battlefield. But the reserves had been held too far back to exploit these early successes. By the time they were able to get to the front, the Germans had greatly strengthened their defences and the eventual attack by the reserves failed.

Although they had been in France only around three weeks, both the untried 24th and 21st Divisions had to endure several exhausting night marches in full kit to arrive at the front. The conditions during their final approach march on the night before the battle were particularly wretched. The narrow roads were packed with traffic and they were constantly held up and, in the confusion, many of the troops arrived late and dead-tired at their allotted areas. During the journey, Richard's brigade, the 73rd, were detached from the rest of the 24th Division and led off to provide reinforcements for the 9th (Scottish) Division at the Hohenzollern Redoubt. Inexplicably, at this vitally critical moment, the C.O. of the 12th Royal Fusiliers was called up to divisional headquarters, leaving Major Garnons-Williams to take over command just before they were ordered to replace the 8th Black Watch at Fosse 8. As they approached the front on the evening of 25 September, they encountered many obstacles and, in the confusion and darkness, the battalion became split up, so the now Acting Lieutenant Colonel Garnons-Williams carried out the initial relief with less than half his men. Going into the line immediately alongside them were the 7th Northamptonshires, which the famous England international Edgar Mobbs had helped to raise. Mobbs survived the carnage of Loos only to die leading his battalion in 1917 at Third Ypres.

Just as the relief was underway, the Germans launched a counter-attack but this was successfully repulsed. For the next two days, the 12th Royal Fusiliers were continually shelled. They had no sleep, no supplies, no water and little food, but, despite their inexperience, they determinedly managed to keep the enemy at bay. However, on 27 September the Germans launched a heavy bombardment and then attacked in strength and began to drive the exhausted British from their hard-won positions. Under attack from their flanks, the Fusiliers were forced to retire back to the Redoubt. Their losses at Loos had been heavy and they suffered 265 casualties.

There is some confusion over the exact date of Richard's death. Most official records give this as 25 September 1915 and the regimental history agrees, saying that he was killed on the day he led his troops into the front line. However, a letter sent to his widow by one of his men strongly suggests that he may have died two days later on 27 September. The circumstances described there do appear to be consistent with the battalion's experiences that particular day.

According to the letter, on 27 September his battalion were at the furthest point they had captured but the position had become untenable and they were forced to retire to straighten the line. The supports on both the right and left had already fallen back, leaving the Fusiliers "in the air" and being enfiladed from their flanks. Tragically, just as Richard was organising the retirement, he was shot in the head and killed instantaneously. The letter concluded:

> I was very sorry for him, as we could not have had a better, braver officer. He was with us all the time in the front trench and looked after us as well as he could; no man could have done better. Nobody could get back to him.

His body was never recovered and identified, so he is now one of the 20,000 men commemorated on the Loos Memorial to the Missing.

Loos Memorial.   [The War Graves Photographic Project]

He was the second of six Newport RFC internationals to die. Since he represented the club at both rugby and cricket, RDG Williams's name should be on the Rodney Parade war memorial, but it is not there. Evidently, he played for Newport so long before the war that the officials responsible for compiling the club's roll of honour were simply unaware of his membership. Nevertheless, his name can be found on memorials around the country, including those at Magdalen College School, Oxford; Trinity College, Cambridge; the Inner Temple; Hay-on-Wye; and, of course, the Millennium Stadium.

The conditions suffered by the men of the 12th Battalion The Royal Fusiliers leading up to and during the Battle of Loos were utterly deplorable. Even for the young and fit, they would have been difficult enough to endure, but it is hard to imagine what it must have been like for someone approaching sixty with the responsibility for the whole battalion suddenly thrust upon his shoulders just as they were going into action. This required a very special kind of heroism. After all, a family man of fifty-nine didn't have to be there, but his unshakeable sense of duty drove him on. Under the most trying of circumstances, he put his men first and, in so doing, Richard Davies Garnons-Williams sacrificed his own life.

"No man could have done better."

Loos Memorial.   [The War Graves Photographic Project]

Charles Gerald Taylor

Born: Ruabon 8 May 1863.
Killed in action: Dogger Bank 24 January 1915.

Teams: HMS Marlborough; Royal Naval College, Greenwich; Blackheath; London Welsh; South Wales.

Wales: 9 caps, 1884-1887.

Just before midday on 23 January 1915, Admiral Sir Arthur Wilson burst into Winston Churchill's office at the Admiralty and exclaimed, "First Lord, those fellows are coming out again!" "Those fellows" were a German squadron under Rear Admiral Hipper and they were "coming out" into the North Sea to harass British light forces in the Dogger Bank area. This news, and the Royal Navy's swift response to it, was to result in the largest naval clash of the Great War so far. It would also claim the life of the first Welsh rugby international to die.

In the modern game, winning nine caps in one season, let alone in a career, might be regarded as nothing special. Yet when Charles Gerald Taylor retired in 1887, only three men had played more times for Wales. Appropriately for a naval officer, he was described as the "sheet anchor" of the Welsh team, as for four seasons he was an automatic choice at three-quarter, missing only one game when he was in hospital. He seems to have been well-liked in rugby circles. Years after his death, *The Times* rugby correspondent recalled him as "a man of charming disposition." Admittedly, his time in the Welsh jersey was not one of great success for Wales. There were no Triple Crowns or Championships but two wins out of two against Ireland and draws with England and Scotland were indications that Wales were never again going to be the push-over they had been when RDG Williams played in 1881. Even though the national team's performances were moderate during the 1880s, it was a seminal decade in the development of the domestic game.

This was when interest in rugby in Wales exploded, with huge increases in the numbers both playing and watching. Around that time, the culture of rugby in Wales also changed irrevocably as the sport began to reach out to the working-class. Such was the growing level of enthusiasm that the south Wales press was already referring to rugby as the national game.

Beginning his international career only three years after RDG Williams, Charles was the fourth oldest of all the 135 rugby internationals who died in the war.[1] Born in 1863, he had a comfortable middle-class upbringing and attended Ruabon Grammar School, where his father Reverend Alfred Taylor was headmaster. Accounts of Charles's rugby career – as well as the official WRU player listings – invariably show "Ruabon" as one of his club affiliations.[2] However, it is extremely doubtful that there was ever a rugby club in the town during his time. Whereas rugby was then already overwhelmingly the choice of footballers in south

Ruabon War Memorial lychgate, St. Mary's Church.   [Siân Prescott]

Wales, there can be no doubt that in the north it was association football which dominated, almost to the total exclusion of any other version. Indeed, Ruabon was a very important early centre of soccer. It was the home of the "father of Welsh football", Llewelyn Kenrick, Welsh soccer's equivalent to rugby's Richard Mullock. A founder of the Football Association of Wales, he organised the first Welsh soccer international and even went one better than Mullock by actually playing for Wales five times between 1876 and 1881. Also, Kenrick just happened to be Charles's brother-in-law, so there must have been some interesting conversations when the families got together. Moreover, Ruabon was also the home of the Druids, the strongest soccer club in Wales at the time. Apart from Bangor, which was founded in 1876 to play rugby, but switched to soccer a year later, and the similarly short-lived Denbigh, founded in 1880, there was very little rugby played in north Wales during Taylor's time.

But, in any case, even if there *had* been a rugby club in Ruabon, Charles

---

1   Those who died at an older age were RDG Williams (59), William Hallaran (Ireland) (55) and Rupert Inglis (England) (53). Inglis was actually two weeks younger than Charles Taylor but he was killed nineteen months after Charles's death.

2   The press also sometimes erroneously reported his club as Wrexham or Bangor.

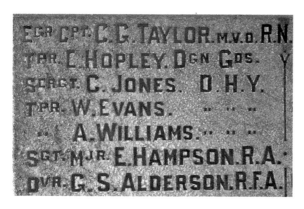

Ruabon's war dead are commemorated on panels in the lychgate. [Siân Prescott]

could not have played for them, because he left his Denbighshire home when he was only sixteen. In July 1879, with his mind firmly set on a naval career, he enrolled as an engineering student at HMS Marlborough in Portsmouth. This was an old 131-gun wooden three-decker, which had been converted in 1877 into accommodation for students who were undergoing training in the workshops at the naval dockyard. The training of all naval engineering officers was later transferred to a new purpose-built Royal Naval Engineering College at Keyham, Devonport and, towards the end of Charles's career, he was placed in command of the college for a short period.

Charles was another sporting all-rounder, who was good at athletics – it is claimed he was the unofficial Welsh pole vault champion at one time – cricket and, in later life, golf. Before he left north Wales, he played soccer for his school and for other local junior teams. At HMS Marlborough, though, the preferred sport was rugby and so it was here that – perhaps with reluctance at first – he was converted into a three-quarter. He soon became a "crack" member of the HMS Marlborough team, where he developed a fine reputation, especially as a kicker. It was a fellow HMS Marlborough student, William Lyne, a brother of the Welsh international and later WRU official, Horace Lyne, who alerted the selectors to Charles's Welsh qualifications. So in November 1883, he was invited, along with Horace Lyne, to play for the South Wales XV against Oxford University. Curiously, several newspapers, including *The Times*, reported his club affiliation as the Druids, believed to be the only occasion when a player in an official WRU team has been listed as belonging to a soccer club! Oxford won by three goals to one, with Charles converting the South Wales try. The twenty-year old had evidently made an impression as, shortly afterwards, he was selected to play on the wing against England at Leeds. Since Godfrey Darbishire (1881) and Charles Allen (1884) were both Lancastrians by birth, he became the second player, after Hugh Vincent (1882), actually born in north Wales to represent his country.

Despite playing all his club rugby outside Wales, Charles was soon acknowledged as a key member of the Welsh back division. In his *Football:*

The Rugby Union Game, published in 1892, Frank Marshall referred to him as:

> one of the most extraordinary players that ever played, as he retained much of his old Association style of play ... (he was) one of the cleverest men in the Kingdom with his feet ... very fast and a good kick.

A useful tackler and not without ability in making ground with the ball in hand, Charles was indeed best known for his kicking, especially his well-executed "flying kicks" to touch.

Then, as now, this was a highly risky tactic but Charles ignored convention and used it to great effect, particularly when dealing with a loose ball or a forward dribble. Years later, youngsters were still being advised, "never fly kick unless you are CG Taylor".

Though he was on the losing side in his first two internationals in 1884, Wales were now demonstrating clear signs of improvement. Charles impressed

Wales v Scotland 1884. Back: H Simpson, F Margrave, WD Phillips; Middle: G Morris, TB Jones, H Lyne, T Clapp, F Andrews, R Gould; Front: C Newman, C Allen, W Gwynn, CP Lewis, CG Taylor, W Norton.   [WRU]

on his debut against England at Leeds and might have immediately elevated himself into the pantheon of Welsh match winners when he attempted a long-range drop goal. Press reports suggest that the ball just swerved outwards over the upright at the last second, but someone with a much better view than the journalists disagreed. The English full-back, HB Tristram, later wrote, "I was standing just in front of the line between the posts when CG Taylor took a drop at goal. The ball passed almost straight over me, about 18 inches *inside* the post." Though the goal was disallowed, Tristram sportingly confessed, "I knew better." So just like HW Thomas twenty-nine years later, Charles came agonisingly close to winning a game, and achieving lasting fame, with a drop goal on his first international appearance.

His second international against Scotland at Newport also ended in defeat, though there were disputes over both the Scottish scores; while Charles dealt coolly with their frequent forward rushes with his trademark flying kicks. So with Wales becoming more competitive, the next match on 12 April 1884 was anticipated with some optimism. This was the occasion of the first visit to Wales by Ireland and it was also the first ever international held at Cardiff Arms Park. In some ways though, the presence of Cardiff's peerless half-back, William "Buller" Stadden, was of even greater historic significance. The first working-class player to represent Wales, his selection demonstrated that thereafter Welsh rugby would no longer be the sole preserve of the socially elite.

Whatever the criticisms of Richard Mullock with regard to the 1881 international with England, there can be little doubt that the selection of the Irish XV which played in Cardiff in 1884 was a far more shambolic affair. It seems there was no great enthusiasm in Ireland for the fixture. A team was selected ten days before the match but only eleven players could be named and of these only nine eventually played. So desperate were the Irish RFU that they were forced to publish a humiliating request in the press inviting interested players ("especially forwards") to contact the Union within three days! Even this didn't help much as, in the end, only twelve players travelled. So the Irish RFU secretary, Herbert Cook, was forced to turn out for his only cap, while two Welsh players, Frank Purdon and Charles Jordan were also drafted in as replacements. To add to the confusion, some of the Irishmen appeared under assumed names. For instance, to prevent his father finding out that he was neglecting his studies, William Hallaran of Dublin University, played as "R.O.N. Hall". Like Charles Taylor, he too was to die during the war when serving as a Colonel in the Royal Army Medical Corps. To this day, there is still disagreement about who actually represented Ireland in Cardiff.

Unsurprisingly, Wales won the match without too much difficulty by

Wales v England 1885. Back: TB Jones, S Goldsworthy, ES Richards; Middle: LC Thomas, H Lyne, T Clapp, JS Smith, R Gould, EM Rowland; Front: H Jordan, CG Taylor, W Gwynn, C Newman, A Gould, F Hancock. [WRU]

a drop goal and two tries to nil. At forward, the Irish did manage to hold their own, no doubt spurred on by Purdon, who had a point to prove, having been discarded by Wales only a couple of months earlier. Behind the scrum, however, the Welsh backs were far superior and "worked together like a machine" with Charles in good form. It would be three years before Ireland would agree to another fixture.

Despite the comprehensive defeat in the next match at the hands of England at Swansea in 1885, Charles was again praised for his defensive play. "Taylor did a lot of good work for Wales, his kicking being of the greatest service", wrote the doyen of English rugby, George Rowland Hill. However, a week later in Glasgow, Wales produced their best result so far when they ground out a nil-all draw with Scotland. Again, Charles almost snatched a dramatic victory with an excellent drop goal attempt which fell just short of the crossbar.

Up to now, Charles had been playing all his club rugby for HMS Marlborough. However, after completing his six-year course at Portsmouth, he was selected for further training at the Royal Naval College, Greenwich. When not turning out for the college he was now able to play at a much higher standard for one of the leading clubs in the land. In October 1885,

"Old Stager" of the *South Wales Daily News* reported that the "sterling Welsh three-quarter C.G. Taylor has, I see, joined the Blackheath ranks". While at Greenwich, Charles was also involved in setting up the London Welsh club and he represented them in their inaugural fixture in October 1885, as well as on other occasions from time to time. However, his main club was Blackheath and being a regular member of this powerful team would have done no harm to his chances of further Welsh caps. In November, Blackheath travelled to Newport, where he helped them overcome a strong South Wales team. A reference to Charles amusing the teams with his banjo at the post-match dinner provides a rare newspaper glimpse into his personality. Evidence that he was now regarded as a senior player was demonstrated following that year's trial when the selectors consulted him on the line-up for the England match at Blackheath in January 1886.

Although most match reports and records list him on the wing, "Old Stager" was certain that Charles played at centre for this game and he was of the opinion that it was a "huge mistake". He made few attempts to run with the ball and his passing to the wings Billy Douglas and Arthur Gould was poor. Perhaps disconcerted by this, even Charles's kicking sometimes let him down and he failed to find touch on a number of occasions. One

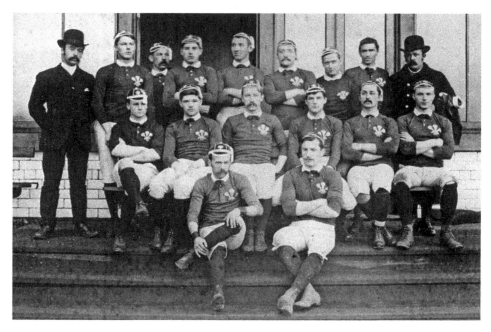

Wales v Scotland 1885. Back: E Alexander, S Goldsworthy, AF Hill, WH Thomas, T Clapp, CG Taylor, D Morgan; Middle: H Jordan, LC Thomas, C Newman, A Gould, F Hancock, R Gould: Front: W Gwynn, TB Jones. [WRU]

miss-kick cost Wales the match, when he sent the ball straight into the arms of the English forward, Charles Elliott, who marked it near half-way. As was permitted in 1886, Elliott handed the ball to his team-mate, Andrew Stoddart, who landed a beautiful long-range goal from the mark. England eventually won by a goal and two tries to a goal. Under the then scoring system, had Stoddart not kicked that goal, Wales would have been the victors. There was some consolation for Charles, however, when he recorded his only score for Wales with a conversion of Stadden's brilliant try.

Following this defeat, the selectors decided to try out the four three-quarter system which, under the leadership of Frank Hancock, was then being exploited by Cardiff with what can only be described as astonishing success. It was a revolutionary system which, for the first time, handed the attacking thrust to the backs, who now concentrated on moving the ball to the wings quickly and accurately, rather than adopting a largely defensive tackling or kicking role. So on 9 January 1886, the first ever international four three-quarter line-up took the field at Cardiff against Scotland. Following his disappointing display at Blackheath, Charles was restored to the wing and he seemed to be happier back in his usual position. Frank Hancock was brought in to partner Arthur Gould at centre, with Billy Douglas completing the history-making quartet. Wales, however, lost by two goals and a try to nil.

Accounts of this match invariably state that the experiment was a failure and certainly Wales abandoned it for the next three years. The secret of Cardiff's success with four three-quarters and eight forwards was combination and precision underscored by regular practice, but this was more difficult to achieve with what was effectively a scratch XV. The Cardiff system relied on forwards who, though one man lighter than their opponents, would concentrate on delivering quick ball to their backs. But the Welsh pack were unable to perform this role effectively and so, at half-time, Wales reverted to three three-quarters, with Harry Bowen being pushed up into the forwards and Gould replacing him at full-back. However, "Old Stager" argued that the system *had* worked well in the first half and Wales should have stuck to it. He claimed the character of the game changed in the second half after Wales retreated to the traditional line-up. Bowen, he felt, made little difference to the pack while his removal from the backs left Wales more exposed behind. He pointed out that Scotland scored only one try in the first half but two in the second. Whatever the truth, it was certainly a disappointing result in front of what was, for those days, an immense crowd confident that Wales would replicate Cardiff's ground-breaking achievements with four three-quarters. That, however, would have to wait just a few more years. To increase capacity, rows of wagons had been placed behind the ropes so that more spectators could view the play. And there were plenty of free-riders watching from the Westgate Street wall and from the windows of surrounding buildings. Charles made some good breaks and he gave the Welsh supporters some brief hope on one occasion, when he almost brought off a sensational score. Receiving a pass from Stadden on the half-way line, he ran through the entire Scottish defence only to have the ball knocked out of his hands in a desperate final tackle as he flung himself over the goal-line. Despite the result, Charles had one of his better games for Wales and he and Gould were credited with saving them from a heavier defeat.

The following season, Wales reverted to three three-quarters and in the fixture with England at Llanelli and they achieved their best international result so far with a scoreless draw. Part of the Stradey pitch was frozen so the game was switched to the adjoining cricket field. On a very hard surface, Wales had the better of the match and Charles was again on form with his kicking, while his tackling was "exceedingly effective". He missed the Scotland game through injury but returned for his final international appearance on 12 March 1887 at Birkenhead Park. Bizarrely this was a home game for Wales and, perhaps even more curiously, it resulted in a Welsh victory, even though they only managed a single try and a drop goal to Ireland's three tries. However, despite playing particularly well and helping Wales achieve their highest placing in the Championship so far – finishing second to Scotland – there was to be no place for serious rugby in Charles's life from now on.

Charles Taylor in naval uniform.

Just three months after winning his last cap, Assistant Engineer Taylor was posted to HMS Carysfort in the Mediterranean where he spent the next three years until he was invalided home with malaria. There then followed a period on the China station, when he managed to find time to play cricket for Hong Kong. He married in 1896 and later had two daughters and a son, Philip, who followed him into the navy and who also served in the Great War, subsequently rising to the rank of Rear Admiral. From 1898, Charles spent five years at the Halifax Naval Dockyard in Nova Scotia, where he was Chief Engineer, a position of considerable responsibility. Returning to England in 1903, Charles held various posts

HMS Tiger depicted on a postcard.

at the Royal Naval Colleges at Osborne and Dartmouth, followed by service in the Home Fleet. An able and efficient officer, he gradually rose through the ranks, eventually being promoted to Engineer-Captain in 1912, a year after being appointed a Member of the Royal Victorian Order (MVO) for his work on developing the training of naval officers. Then in August 1913, he was placed in command of the Royal Naval Engineering College, Keyham where no doubt he took more than a passing interested in the performances of the rugby XV. However, this was a brief appointment for, with the outbreak of the war, he was immediately posted to the battle cruiser HMS Queen Mary. Here he served on the staff of Rear Admiral Sir David Beatty as his engineering adviser. Beatty was then in command of the First Battle Cruiser Squadron and in late November 1914, Engineer-Captain Taylor was transferred to HMS Tiger, a brand new ship which had just joined this squadron.

Unknown to the Germans, the British had been intercepting their radio traffic and breaking into their naval codes. So less than two hours after Rear Admiral Hipper received his instructions to sweep into the Dogger Bank area, this information was also in the hands of the Admiralty. Hipper left Wilhelmshaven on the evening of 23 January 1915, with three battle cruisers and a large but fatally slower armoured cruiser, SMS Blücher. They were accompanied by four light cruisers and eighteen destroyers. Responding immediately, Churchill despatched Beatty from Rosyth with a force of five powerful battle cruisers, including HMS Tiger, and four light cruisers. In addition, from the south, a flotilla of three light cruisers and thirty-five destroyers set out from Harwich and they met up with Beatty north of Dogger Bank on the morning of 24 January. Soon the German ships were sighted.

Charles Taylor's grave marker at Tavistock Cemetery. [The War Graves Photographic Project]

After the first contact, a surprised Hipper immediately turned his smaller squadron around and raced for home and safety. The operation now became a fast-moving, running battle which lasted several hours. Eventually, three of Beatty's battle cruisers, Lion, Tiger and Princess Royal began to close on the German squadron, at the rear of which was the straggling Blücher. Before long, all three British ships opened fire on her and she was eventually sunk with the loss of up to a thousand lives. However, confusion over Beatty's signals resulted in the British ships continuing to concentrate on sinking the disabled Blücher, rather than moving on to engage the rest of the German squadron, which managed to escape. So the opportunity for a major British success was missed. Nevertheless, since no Royal Navy ships were lost, Dogger Bank was considered a British victory and it was, therefore, a great morale booster at this early stage of the war.

Victory or opportunity lost, it made little difference to the families of the fifteen Royal Navy personnel who died in the battle. Though Beatty's flagship HMS Lion had been badly damaged and put out of action, it was HMS Tiger which suffered most of the British losses at Dogger Bank. According to one witness, a heavy shell exploded in a compartment below Tiger's signal bridge, killing all those inside. Charles, who was acting as a spotting officer, had been standing outside near a steel hatchway which had inadvertently been left open. Caught in the blast from the explosion, he was killed instantly. Fifty-one year-old Engineer-Captain Charles Taylor was the only officer fatality on the British side. His body was taken back to Rosyth and then on to his home in Devon for burial in Tavistock New Cemetery. The war was just over five months old, yet fourteen rugby internationals from France, Scotland and England had already made the supreme sacrifice.[1] The Battle of Dogger Bank now added the first Welshman to the game's roll of honour.

Charles Taylor's grave marker. [The War Graves Photographic Project]

---

1 They were: Joseph Anduran, Emmanuel Iguinitz, Gaston Lane, Alfred Mayssonnié, François Poydebasque (France); James Huggan, Lewis Robertson, James Ross, Ronald Simson, Frederic Turner (Scotland); Francis Oakley, James Watson, Charles Wilson (England); and Sidney Crowther (Great Britain).

Louis Augustus Phillips

Born: Newport 24 February 1878.
Killed in action: Cuinchy 14 March 1916.

Teams: Monmouth School; Newport.

Wales: 4 caps, 1900-1901.

As a small, somewhat reticent and self-effacing half-back ran onto the field at Kingsholm, Gloucester to win his first cap, he would not have known that he was about to participate in the beginning of one of the greatest periods of Welsh international rugby. Some people dispute whether the twentieth century began in 1900 or 1901, but there can be little disagreement that 6 January 1900 marked the dawn of a new era for the Welsh game.

This was another significant turning point in the history of Welsh rugby. During the previous nineteen years, Wales managed to win only sixteen of their forty-six fixtures and they achieved the Triple Crown only once. Over the twelve seasons from 1899-1900 to 1910-11, in what became known as the first "Golden Era", Wales would play forty-three matches and lose only seven. There were victories over New Zealand and Australia, while in thirteen meetings with England between 1899 and 1911 they lost only once. They won six Triple Crowns and, with France coming into the Championship in 1908, the last three of these were converted into Grand Slams. The basis of this success was the "Welsh game", the Cardiff four three-quarter passing game, now at last firmly hitched to a powerful pack of forwards. However, although "Lou" Phillips's contribution to the "Golden Era" was to be a distinguished one, it was also brief. Wretched bad luck meant that, after the 1900 Triple Crown, Lou would play no further part in these successes. As a consequence, his role in the story has been largely over-looked.

When the *South Wales Argus* reported his death in 1916, the headline announced "Great Athlete Killed". This was no journalistic exaggeration. After all, Lou had been one of the most talented all-rounders in pre-war Wales. Yet, even though he represented Newport at five different sports and was a double – and probably a triple – Welsh international, Lou was always extremely modest about his sporting achievements.

As shown earlier, the title of this book is taken from a passage in WJ Townsend Collins's fascinating *"Rugby Recollections"* published in 1948. It can be found in his reminiscences about one particular player, who even then was fading from popular memory:

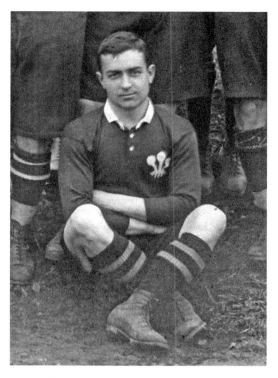

> Football memories are short. Players whose names should be written in gold in the annals of football are forgotten or half-forgotten: it is a pious duty to call them to remembrance. There may be a few outside his native town who still

Lou Phillips on his debut for Wales.

speak with admiration of L.A. ("Lou") Phillips, the half-back who was associated with G. Llewellyn Lloyd for Newport and Wales from 1897 till 1901.

Because Lou's international career lasted for only a year, his reputation has undoubtedly been overshadowed by the great Welsh half-backs of his era like the James brothers and Dicky Owen. Even so, Townsend Collins regarded Lou as one of the best Welsh half-backs he had seen in his sixty years of reporting on the game. Such expert opinion from one of the most experienced rugby writers of the time cannot be discounted lightly.

Lou's trophy cabinet must have been a big one. He was a decent Newport club cricketer and even represented Monmouthshire in the Minor Counties Championship once – though admittedly not with much success – against Glamorgan at the Arms Park in 1899. He was a particularly fine competitive swimmer. On at least two occasions during the 1890s he won the annual one mile River Usk race. A powerful swimmer as well as a resilient ball-player, he was a natural for the highly physical demands of water-polo.

In 1897, he not only helped Newport win the Welsh Championship but ended the season as the tournament's top goal scorer. Some sources suggest that he represented Wales at water-polo. Whilst this has proved difficult to confirm – especially as the Welsh Amateur Swimming Association's records are incomplete – one contemporary newspaper report reveals that he was a reserve for Wales on one occasion, so he was certainly at least very close to international standard.

Lou was also a very proficient golfer, but it was for rugby football that he first became widely known. The son of a prominent Newport corn merchant, Lou was born in 1878 at Stow Hill in the heart of the rapidly expanding town. When he was thirteen, Lou began boarding at Monmouth School, where he soon became recognised as one of the school's greatest pre-war sportsmen and where he first demonstrated his exceptional talent for rugby. Possessing "a short but very powerful frame, sound hands and great kicking power, cool and quick judgement, (and) a fearless and imperturbable temper", according to the school magazine, he was a member of the school's strongest XV of the period. The 1894 side was brimming with talent and besides Lou it included two other future internationals in Reg Skrimshire of Wales and Philip Nicholas who, despite being born in Monmouth, played for England. Lou left Monmouth in 1895 and was articled to a firm of architects in Newport, eventually qualifying in 1907, after which he practised independently. He joined Newport RFC soon after leaving school, playing at half-back initially for the Third XV. Gradually gaining experience, he finally broke into the First XV in October 1897 when a mere youngster of nineteen. He had an impressive debut against Blackheath and immediately established himself as the regular Newport half-back. From then on, over four seasons Lou missed only four First XV fixtures (twice when playing for Wales) and represented the club in ninety matches in all.

During his first season, he struck up a wonderful half-back partnership with G. Llewellyn Lloyd, who won twelve caps for Wales between 1896 and 1903. The two men quickly developed an uncanny, almost perfect, understanding of each other's play. They were both "half-backs" rather than scrum-half and fly-half, and in each match they would share the duties of "working the scrum" or playing outside, depending on the circumstances. The division into specialised inside- and outside-halves was only beginning to emerge at this time, but Lloyd and Phillips could and did play equally well at both. Townsend Collins was unequivocal about Lloyd. He was "the best half-back I have ever seen". But he greatly admired Phillips too. He recalled that "in 1899-1900 they were the half-backs of the season. There were few more brilliant individuals – there certainly was no pair, club or international, who were so thoroughly effective."

Cool and unflappable in a crisis and possessing a "never say die" temperament, Lou was an asset for any side. He was a strong and determined runner, he gave and took passes well, and tackled robustly and kicked accurately. But he had no tricks or subtleties. Townsend Collins says that neither he nor Lloyd introduced any new moves like Swansea's Dicky Owen and Dick Jones.

Monmouth School War Memorial.   [Gwyn Prescott]

Nevertheless, Lou "played the orthodox game of the day with great success" and he "was one of those great-hearted players who refuse to give up even when the position seems hopeless."

After playing together for two seasons, the Newport pair were chosen for the England match at Gloucester. The Welsh press were optimistic about their prospects and they were not disappointed. Wales comfortably defeated England by 13 points to 3. One of the try scorers was Dick Hellings of Llwynypia, who played most of the game with a fractured arm. Such stoicism was not uncommon then, as will shortly be seen. Lou was a great success in both attack and defence. "Old Stager" described him as one of the best of the Welsh backs, adding that at half-back, there was only one side in it. *The Sportsman* newspaper agreed, acknowledging that Lloyd and Phillips continually outwitted and outplayed the English half-backs.

It was a similar story when Scotland came to Swansea three weeks later. In front of a huge 40,000 crowd, the Newport half-backs again excelled in all phases of the game. "Old Stager" wrote, "while the defence of both was sound, Lloyd's cleverness in resource and his dodging ability was equalled by the splendid fielding and screw-kicking to touch by Phillips". Again, they "completely out manoeuvred" their opposing half-backs. With Gwyn Nicholls returning to the three-quarter line after a prolonged stay in Australia following the Great Britain tour, Wales dominated the game and scored four tries to one, winning 12-3. One of Willie Llewellyn's two tries was started by Lou when he outsmarted the Scottish halves at a scrum

Wales v England 1900. Back: WH Williams, J Blake, G Boots, W Millar, J Hodges, A Brice; Second Row: R Hellings, D Rees, G Davies, W Trew; Third Row: W Llewellyn, W Bancroft; Front: R Thomas, GL Lloyd, LA Phillips.   [Gloucester RFC]

deep in Welsh territory. It was a cracker. Lou confused his opponents by appearing to make a break but then passed out to Lloyd. The ball then went through the hands of Billy Trew, George Davies and Gwyn Nicholls who, after one of his famous swerving runs, passed to the Llwynypia winger, Willie Llewellyn, just over the half-way line. He then outpaced the remaining Scottish defence to score one of the most spectacular tries seen at St. Helens up to then.

So then it was off to Balmoral in Belfast for the final international of the 1899-1900 season. It was a rough crossing and a tough match, characterised by deadly tackling on both sides. But the imperturbable Lou Phillips was in his element. Lloyd was injured so Selwyn Biggs of Cardiff replaced him in Welsh XV. The pair played with a greater degree of cohesion than expected, though "the perfect combination" with Lloyd was undeniably missed. In the end, this gruelling match was won by a single score and again Lou had a hand in it. "Phillips's part in the try was as clever a bit as contributed by the halves", wrote "Old Stager". Taking the ball from Alf Brice at a line-out, Lou made a determined break upfield, eventually transferring to Gwyn

Nicholls who, now going at full tilt, beat his man and gave a perfectly timed pass to George Davies, who ran in for the try. The Swansea centre was concussed by a kick to the mouth as he went over and only knew that he had scored after he was revived. Billy Bancroft's conversion failed but the 3-0 score-line was sufficient for victory.

Today there is a trophy for any side which defeats the other three "home nations" in one season. In 1900, however, winning was reward enough. "Old Stager" reminded his readers that Wales had won, "what has come to be generally spoken of as the triple crown – a jewelled headgear which only exists in fancy". It was, nevertheless, a magnificent achievement – only once before in 1893 had Wales managed it – and Lou Phillips was at the heart of this success.

There was no doubt that he would retain his place in the Welsh XV the following season. But, playing in a Christmas fixture with Cork Constitution at Rodney Parade, Lou suffered a bad knee injury late in the game. Moments before, he and Lloyd had participated in some classic inter-passing which resulted in Lloyd scoring Newport's fifth try. Regrettably though, this would be the last time that rugby supporters would witness these two half-backs working their magic together. Years later, Lloyd would describe Lou's injury as a major catastrophe for Newport at the time. Undefeated until February, they lost only twice in 1900-1 but still missed out on the Welsh Championship by the narrowest of margins. "He was at the height of his playing career and his loss was irreplaceable. The vital link between forwards and three-quarters was broken".

The England game at Cardiff was held only nine days after the Cork match. Lou was selected but his injury hadn't recovered and so, on the morning of the match, he cried off. John "Bala" Jones of Aberavon came in as his replacement for his only cap. Wales deservedly won 13-0 but did not play particularly well. The *Western Mail* felt Lou had been missed, referring to him as "certainly the best defensive half back that Wales has today". The selectors were understandably anxious to see Lou return to the team and, perhaps unwisely, they picked him for the next fixture against Scotland at Inverleith on 9 February 1901. *The Times* certainly expected his return to strengthen the Welsh XV and predicted another win for Wales. Lou had been given a little more time to recover by the death of Queen

Newport Athletic Club War Memorial, Rodney Parade. *[Siân Prescott]*

Victoria which had resulted in the postponement of the game. However, this was not of much benefit to him as he broke down completely when the match was only ten minutes old. It would be nearly seventy years before substitutes were allowed so, although Lou was incapacitated and in some pain, he remained on the pitch throughout. Here we see evidence of that spirit, determination and "never say die temperament" for which he was renowned. Although he was now little more than a passenger and unable to contribute much to the cause, he bravely carried on and, in so doing, caused lasting damage to his knee. Strangely, the Welsh captain, Billy Bancroft was reluctant to move Lou out and so he left him dangerously exposed in the pivotal position of half-back. After the match, Bancroft was criticised for this unaccountable failure. It was a grave mistake and a situation too good to miss for the Scots. With the ruthless David Bedell-Sivright in his customary uncompromising and predatory form, they exploited the break-down at half-back and went on to win easily by 18 points to 8.[1]

Not only was this Lou's last game for Wales, it was his last game of rugby. He was only twenty-two. We can only speculate what further career Lou might have enjoyed had he not suffered that injury. Would more Welsh honours have followed or would he have inevitably soon lost his place to the far more innovative Dicky Owen? We shall never know. What is incontrovertible is that Owen replaced him for the final match that season against Ireland and he never looked back, going on to win a record thirty-five caps for Wales and in so doing establish himself as one of the undoubted all-time greats of the game. The devastating knee injury was not, however, the end of Lou's sporting life, because he soon turned his attention to golf with remarkable success.

His rise to prominence in this sport was considered "meteoric" by the golfing press. He was the Newport club champion on several occasions and he also set a new club course record. Only four years after taking up the game, despite never having had a lesson, he won the Welsh Amateur Golf Championship at Porthcawl in 1907 at his first attempt. Lou repeated this triumph with another victory in the 1912 Welsh Championship, again held at Porthcawl, when he defeated rugby international Bert Winfield in the quarter-final. More honours followed. A month later both men played for the first ever representative Welsh team against the Midlands, whom

---

1   Bedell-Sivright was one of the larger-than-life characters of rugby in the first decade of the century, winning twenty-two caps for Scotland and taking part in two British Lions tours, captaining the 1904 team in Australia and New Zealand. A surgeon in the Royal Naval Division, he died of blood poisoning at Gallipoli in September 1915.

1912 Welsh Golf Championship semi-finalists: A. Smith, HB Rowley, LA Phillips and Cyril Turnbull. Lou Phillips (Newport Golf Club) defeated Turnbull (Glamorganshire Golf Club) 4 and 3 in the final.

they defeated 5-4 at Southerndown. Spurred on by this success, the Welsh Golfing Union arranged their first (and only pre-war) international match against Ireland in September 1913. Wales lost 6 and ½ to 8 and ½, but Lou won his singles defeating HA Boyd, one of the best Irish golfers and, with Bert Winfield as his partner, halved the foursomes. Staying on a few days to compete in the Irish Amateur Open at Dollymount, he played brilliantly to become the first Welshman to reach the final. Despite being firm favourite though, he did not do justice to himself and he failed to take the title. Entering the 1914 Open Amateur Championship held in May that year at Sandwich, he again performed extraordinarily well, reaching the last eight. After he had defeated his fifth round opponent – who had previously knocked out the 1913 Open Champion – *The Times* reported that "Mr. Phillips has a firm, crisp decided way of playing his iron clubs and a confident style of putting ... (he) is a good golfer and, as befitting one used to Welsh football crowds, a hard fighter". Sadly, this was to be Lou's last appearance in a major tournament. He was chosen to captain Wales in the return match with Ireland but this was never played because it had been arranged for August 1914.

At the time hostilities broke out, Lou was still a bachelor and enjoying an agreeable lifestyle in Newport. He was a successful architect and a much admired sportsman, still bringing distinction to his home town. He was now thirty-six and getting on a bit for military life, but duty called and Lou did not hold back. A month after the declaration of war, he gave up the comfort of his life in Newport to enlist in the 20th (Service) Battalion (3rd Public Schools) The Royal Fusiliers. This unit's secondary title reflected its origin as one of the four battalions raised in September 1914 by the "Public Schools and University Men's Force". Given their background, many of the recruits later became officers (as did Johnny Williams) but Lou refused a commission, though he did eventually accept promotion to sergeant. Had he survived the Western Front for longer than four months, it is possible that he would have been unable to resist further calls to take up a commission.

The 20th Royal Fusiliers first trained at Leatherhead, then moved to Clipstone in Nottinghamshire and finally to Tidworth on Salisbury Plain. Lou landed in France on 15 November 1915 with his battalion who were now allocated to the 19th Brigade, 33rd Division. They spent their first six months of war gaining experience on the La Bassée sector. This was not an easy introduction to the realities of trench warfare. The conditions were wet and muddy and there were not only trench raids to contend with but also the additional terrors of mining and countermining.

One of the four infantry battalions in the 19th Brigade were the Regulars of the 2nd Battalion The Royal Welsh Fusiliers and one of the old sweats in this battalion was Private Frank Richards from Blaina, who later wrote the First World War classic, "Old Soldiers Never Die". In common with many Regulars, he did not have a high opinion of some of the volunteers. He

UNIVERSITY & PUBLIC SCHOOLS BRIGADE

5000 MEN AT ONCE

The Old Public School and University Men's Committee makes an urgent appeal to their fellow Public School and University men to at once enlist in these battalions, thus upholding the glorious traditions of their Public Schools & Universities.

TERMS OF SERVICE.

Age on enlistment 1 ... soldiers up to 35 and certain ex-non-commissioned off ... up to 50. Height 5 ft. 3 in. and upwards. Chest 34 in. at least. ... be medically fit

General Service for the War.

Men enlisting for the duration of the War will be discharged with all convenient speed at the conclusion of the War

PAY AT ARMY RATES.

and all married men or widowers with children will be accepted, and will draw separation allowance under Army Conditions

HOW TO JOIN.

Men wishing to join should apply at once, personally, to the Public Schools & Universities Force, 66, Victoria Street, Westminster, London, S.W., or the nearest Recruiting Office of this Force.

GOD SAVE THE KING !

Recruiting poster for the University and Public Schools Brigade, which Lou joined in September 1914.

wrote that the Royal Fusiliers "were very decent chaps" but was rather scathing about them as soldiers. He noted that their mail was twice as large as that of the rest of the brigade but was particularly impressed with their proficiency at swearing.

On 12 March 1916, after a period of rest in billets, the 20th Royal Fusiliers were ordered back into the firing line north-west of Loos near the La Bassée Canal at Cuinchy. They barely had time to settle into front line routine when the Germans blew a mine near their trenches. Fortunately this caused no immediate casualties but a later enemy bombing (hand-grenade) raid cost the lives of five Fusiliers. However, the raiders were successfully beaten off and the Fusiliers managed to maintain their hold on the lip of the mine crater. Then, on the night of 14 March 1916, Sergeant Lou Phillips was detailed for a wiring party to consolidate the position near the crater when

Lou Phillips in uniform.

Often incorrectly said to have died at Cambrai, Lou Phillips is buried at Cambrin Churchyard Extension near Béthune. [The War Graves Photographic Project]

Louis Augustus Phillips's headstone.   [The War Graves Photographic Project]

the Germans launched another raid. Again this was repulsed but it was probably during this action that Lou was shot in the chest and killed, another brave victim of the casual attrition which was a daily experience of life on the Western Front. He was the only fatality reported in the battalion's War Diary that day.

A little later the battalion's chaplain wrote to Lou's next of kin to tell them that he had been buried not far from where he had died – along with the five Royal Fusiliers killed the day before – in a small churchyard near the front line. To this day – just over a mile from where his fellow Newport clubman and Royal Fusilier, Richard Garnons-Williams fell – Louis Augustus Phillips, Newport's "Great Athlete", still lies with his comrades in the Cambrin Churchyard Extension.

Shortly after his burial in France, the *South Wales Argus* paid a lasting tribute to the deeply modest half-back who had helped usher in Wales's first "Golden Era". Lou Phillips was "one of the most reticent of men and no-one talked less about his athletic achievements; but he was as true as steel, kind-hearted ... a "sportsman" in the best sense of the term."

Charles Meyrick Pritchard

Born: Newport 30 September 1882.
Died of wounds: Chocques 14 August 1916.

Teams: Long Ashton School, Bristol; Newport Thursdays; Newport; Monmouthshire.

Wales: 14 caps, 1904-1910.

"Valiant as a lion; and wondrous affable" was how Shakespeare portrayed Owain Glyndŵr, one the great heroes of Welsh history. It is also an accurate description of another heroic Welshman, Charles Meyrick Pritchard. Frequently referred to as having the courage of a lion, he was also widely admired for his genial, warm-hearted and chivalrous nature.

The English journalist, EHD Sewell, paid him this handsome tribute:

> His ceaseless and quite indefatigable energy was a feature of every match he played in … and he played himself to a standstill in the memorable game with the New Zealanders … He had the true tackle, hard and low, and very tenacious … His game was true as a bell, like his nature, which was unfailingly cheerful and full of exuberance. He made hosts of friends among opponents and fellow-players alike; and although no forward of his day played a game more full of fire, nobody ever saw Charlie Pritchard guilty of anything but the cleanest, straightest Rugby.

His team-mate, George Boots, referred to him as "Charlie of the lion heart … (but) he was very much more than a robust forward. He was chivalrous; he was always generous … Many a time I have seen him stop to pick up an opponent." Townsend Collins recognised the same great-hearted qualities:

> That tremendous strength which laid the New Zealand forwards down

"like skittles" was continually used with a smiling heartiness to lift an opponent who had been laid low ... and never in his whole football career did he play a dirty trick. Vigorous he was but he was always a gentleman on and off the field.

He was a great forward and he was the most loveable of all the Newport captains I have known. On the field he was a lion; off the field he was one of the tenderest ... of men. There was a quality of greatness in his manner ... and as great a player as he was, one thinks of him as a good comrade, a genial companion – "a very gallant gentleman" who laid down his life in the Great War.

Unquestionably one of the great forwards of Welsh rugby, in his long and distinguished career, there is one match above all others with which Charlie Pritchard will always be linked. "Old Stager" rated his contribution to the victory over New Zealand in December 1905 at the highest level: "The names that will be most prominently associated with the match will be Owen, Nicholls, Winfield and the Pritchards." *Fields of Praise* refers to him as the undoubted star of the Welsh pack.

Superbly captained by David Gallaher, the all-conquering All Blacks arrived in Wales with an unblemished record, but now they faced by far the toughest leg of their tour. The match with Wales, it was reckoned, would decide the "rugby championship of the world". With some prescience, "Forward" of the *Western Mail* wrote on the morning of the game that it was the "most fateful of all days in the history of Rugby football" in Wales. This feeling was evident in and around the ground where there was an intense atmosphere unlike anything which those present, including the All Blacks, had ever experienced. Only adding to the fervour, in a precedent-setting stroke of genius, the ritual of the pre-match haka was countered with a highly charged rendition of Hen Wlad Fy Nhadau and a sporting tradition was born.

Newport Athletic Club War Memorial. [Siân Prescott]

The game's only score came after thirty minutes from a well-rehearsed and cleverly executed move. It began with a decoy play which sent most of the All Blacks' defence the wrong way. Then Charlie's cousin, Cliff Pritchard, provided the pivotal link between Dicky Owen and Rhys Gabe, which eventually led to Teddy Morgan's winning try. The match itself was a fierce gladiatorial contest. To Townsend Collins, it seemed that both packs, sometimes ignoring

Wales v New Zealand 1905. Back: JF Williams, G Travers, Dai Jones, W Joseph, R Gabe; Middle: CM Pritchard, J Hodges, W Llewellyn, EG Nicholls, HB Winfield, Cliff Pritchard, A Harding; Front: ET Morgan, R Owen, P Bush.

the laws, were determined to see how much punishment their opponents could survive. Throughout, Charlie's tackling was deadly. "Always in the thick of the fight", he performed "prodigies of aggressive defence". After the game, his team-mate, George Travers, famously acclaimed, "he sent 'em down like ninepins!" And when the Welsh line was under severe pressure near the end of the match, it was none other than the "lion-hearted Charlie Pritchard" who won the ball and "made a great burst and brought relief". Charlie's resolute and unflagging commitment to the cause was summed up in one particularly striking and memorable eulogy: "he took his gruelling like a man."

Charlie came from a sporting family. His father, John Pritchard, was a well-known Newport cricketer and founder member of the Newport Cricket and Football Club. In 1881, he played for a Newport XXII against WG Grace's All-England XI and was invited by Grace to keep wicket for his All-England team, though he was unable to accept. Charlie's brothers, Percy and Ivan, also played for Newport RFC. Charlie briefly attended Newport Intermediate (High) School, a rugby nursery in later years, but at that time a soccer school. Happily for the future of Welsh rugby, Charlie was then sent to Long Ashton, a private school near Bristol, where he was taught the game.

After leaving school, he began working in the family wine and spirit business. At first this restricted his rugby but, while playing for Newport Thursdays, he was spotted by a Newport official and invited to join the town club. So in January 1902, at just nineteen, he was selected reserve for Newport's fixture at Swansea. As luck would have it, a player dropped out and Charlie was in the team. There wasn't a harder place than St. Helens for a young and inexperienced forward to be introduced to the senior game. Swansea were currently enjoying their own "golden era" and had not only been Welsh Champions for three years on the trot, but were still unbeaten that season.

Newport, however, took Swansea's record, winning an exceedingly competitive game 6-3. Completely unfazed by the occasion, the youthful Charlie did so well that, realising that they had a great find on their hands, Newport retained him for the rest of the season. The Black and Ambers lost only three games in 1901-2 and were just pipped for the Championship by Swansea, but they and Charlie had every reason to feel pleased. Apart from two lengthy periods of injury, Charlie remained a permanent and towering presence in the Newport pack until 1911. He appeared for his club 219 times over ten years and was a popular captain for three consecutive seasons (1906-9), though he was injured for much of that time. Johnny Williams was a team-mate in Charlie's first season, while in later years he also played alongside Phil Waller and Billy Geen in Newport colours.

Charlie's first full season for Newport was a very successful one, in which they won the 1902-3 Welsh Championship, losing only twice in thirty-three fixtures. His continuing improvement was now getting noticed and, after appearing for the Possibles in the Welsh trial, he was chosen third forward reserve for Wales in Belfast in March 1904. First, two forwards cried off. Then, on the day before the match, another was taken ill. So against all the odds – nobody could remember it happening before – the third reserve was in the Welsh XV. Charlie was just twenty-one. "Forward" thought that, if anything, he would strengthen the team: "He is young, well-built and full of vim." The match was a thrilling affair. Ireland looked beaten with fifteen minutes to go but they then scored two quick tries and a conversion to take a 14-12 lead. Controversy followed, however. The Scottish referee Findlay Crawford, widely believed to be prejudiced against Wales because they committed the unforgivable sin of selecting working men, disallowed a brilliant last gasp match-winning try by Dick Jones. Crawford was the only person in the ground who saw a forward pass in the move.

Charlie, though, had a good debut. Townsend Collins noted the modesty of the man after he had received the highest praise for his performance that day. "I think I must have done all my good things right under the noses of the Welsh Committee and the Press." From then on, Charlie was an automatic choice for Wales, playing fourteen times over seven seasons, though injury cost him at least another ten caps.

After only three years of senior rugby, Charlie became a Triple Crown player. It began with an astounding win over England in Cardiff by seven tries and two conversions to nil. Amounting to 25-0 at the time, with modern scoring values the margin would have been 39 points, well outstripping the 30-3 victory over England in 2013, widely acclaimed, perhaps unfairly for the men of 1905, as a record score. Then, Scotland were despatched by 6 points to 3 in a bruising battle

Charlie Pritchard.

up front, in which Charlie was conspicuous. Wales went on to take their fourth Triple Crown by beating Ireland 10-3, but without Charlie who had to pull out with a sprained ankle. But even these achievements of 1904-5 could not match what was to come next, with the visit of the All Blacks.

A week after the Welsh triumph over New Zealand, Charlie faced them again for Newport in a game described by David Gallaher as one of the best contested matches of the tour. "Forward" thought the All Blacks only barely deserved their 6-3 win while Charlie was "on the top of his form". The international with England was next up and the confidence of the Welsh team was naturally high. The game took place at Richmond and it gave "Forward" the opportunity to reflect on the differences in attitude between the two countries: "In Wales, Rugby is more than a game. It is a national institution ... our players regard it as the acme of their athletic ambition to win their cap, and those are the secrets of our supremacy". He was critical of the poor attendance and disparaging about the lack of enthusiasm amongst the English supporters. And he must have ruffled a few feathers by patronisingly declaring that England would have to take the game more seriously in future "if they hope to re-gain their position among the four nations". It was another convincing victory for Wales by 16 points to 3, in which the seven-man Welsh pack dominated the English eight, with Charlie Pritchard and Jehoida Hodges the pick of the bunch. Both men scored tries. The seven forwards were retained for Scotland at Cardiff but this time they were bettered by the Scottish pack, though Wales still managed a 9-3 win. A consecutive Triple Crown now beckoned in Ireland, where Dai Westacott won his only cap, but with the Welsh team ravaged by sea-sickness and a rampant Irish XV, all hopes of victory were dashed. So a season which began so well ended with enormous disappointment.

It didn't start any better for Wales in 1906-7 either when South Africa were the visitors. The Springboks had already beaten Newport 8-0 but, with Charlie leading his men in style and revelling in the physical contact, the Black and Amber pack had had the better of the game. So the Welsh forwards were expected to do well too but on the day they displayed an inexplicable lack of spirit. The South Africans completely controlled the match and the unofficial "world champions" went down to a somewhat humiliating 11-0 defeat. It was a chastening experience for new caps Dick Thomas and Johnny Williams, as well as for Charlie, who may well have regretted revealing to the bemused Springboks after the Newport match how the Welsh always managed to gain the loose head at the scrum.

But then the wheel turned again. Wales recovered quickly to record a six try 22-0 romp over England at Swansea, at which the *Western Mail* rejoiced, "Englishmen Routed Fore and Aft". *The Times* acknowledged that "seldom has the victory of a Welsh side over an English side been so complete".

It was back to earth with a bump in Edinburgh, however, where Scotland won the Triple Crown decider 6-3. Playing seven against eight for the last time, the pack managed to hold their own against the powerful Scottish forwards until late on. Charlie though "once again took pride of place". With Percy Bush having a hand in almost all the scores, Ireland were then crushed 29-0 in one of the most accomplished exhibitions ever seen at the Arms Park. The match also witnessed one of Charlie's crunching tackles on Basil Maclear to stop the star Irish wing from scoring. *L'Auto's* rugby correspondent lamented, "I wish we could get such games in France". Mid-career, Charlie was now at the height of his powers. Though for Wales, 1906-7 had been another mixed season, for Charlie personally it had been a great success. In a public poll, he was voted the forward of the year, while his play was summed up thus:

> He has gained steadily in judgement and knowledge of the game; strong as a lion, his dash is tremendous. He gives and takes passes well, his scrimmaging and tackling are great and his dribbling good, and altogether he is a great forward.

His twelfth international in January 1908 proved to be an historic occasion for, in defeating England 28-18, Wales took the lead in the series for the first time. The audacious Percy Bush was again superlative at outside-half but the match is also remembered for the thick fog which covered the Ashton Gate ground. With the players frequently disappearing from

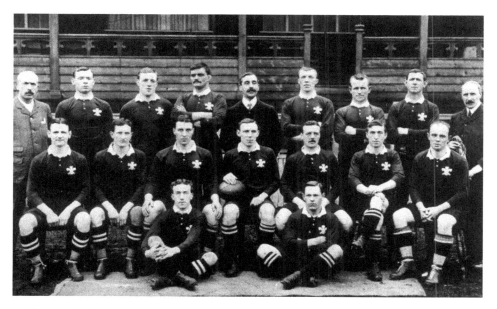

Wales v Ireland 1907. Back: T. Evans, W Dowell, J Brown, W Rees (WRU Secretary), G Travers, J Watts, W O'Neill; Middle: J Evans, DP Jones, CM Pritchard, R Gabe, HB Winfield, JL Williams, A Harding; Front: P Bush, R David.   [WRU]

sight, no-one was able to view the whole match. This was the first leg of another successful Triple Crown (and first Grand Slam) season but a bad knee injury prevented Charlie from taking part in the subsequent victories over Scotland, France and Ireland. "Old Stager" remarked that "his loss was very much felt". He remained injured in 1908-9 too and – a certainty to have been picked otherwise – he missed the defeat of Australia as well as a second Grand Slam. He had to wait two years before wearing the Welsh jersey again in the ten try annihilation of France in Swansea on New Year's Day 1910.

Charlie's fourteenth and final cap came two weeks later in the first ever international held at Twickenham. There was little to choose between the sides. The Welsh pack went well but the backs under-performed. In the end, England gained their first win over Wales in twelve years by 11 points to 6. Charlie was selected for Scotland but his absence may reveal much about his sporting and big-hearted nature. The first reserve was Newport's Ernie Jenkins who had not yet been capped. This season was thought to be Ernie's last chance of international honours, and it was believed by some that Charlie cried off with a rib injury, which was not really serious, to allow Ernie to win his cap. Ernie played well and, following a Welsh victory, he was retained for the Ireland game. Charlie's distinguished international career was over. He played one more season of club rugby and then retired at the end of 1910-11, no doubt looking forward to many years of supporting his beloved Newport and Wales. But the German invasion of Belgium on 4 August 1914 was to deny him that.

On 31 May 1915 Charlie was commissioned Second Lieutenant to the 12th (Service) Battalion (3rd Gwent) The South Wales Borderers which had formed at Newport a little earlier. A month afterwards, they moved to Prees Heath, Shropshire and there Charlie was promoted to lieutenant. In September came another move, this time to Aldershot where the battalion was now allocated to the 40th Division, which was made up mainly of recruits of small stature and hence known as a "Bantam" Division. The 12th SWB was one of the four Welsh battalions in the 119th Brigade and these were comprised mainly of miners who, though generally small, were fit, hardy and tough. However, the other two infantry brigades in the 40th Division included many recruits who were underdeveloped and unfit for active service. As a result, there were long delays in bringing these other two brigades up to establishment and getting them ready for war service.

Promoted captain from the previous November, Charlie eventually went overseas with the 3rd Gwents on 2 June 1916. Sadly his time in France was to be all too brief. His battalion went into intensive training behind the lines near Béthune and on 14 June they received their first taste of trench life under instruction from experienced front line troops. Then on 3 July, they took over part of the Calonne sector and remained in the line between here and Loos for the next four months, before the 40th Division moved down to the Somme, but Charlie never survived long enough to serve there.

This was a period of active patrolling and raiding and it was a raid that cost Charlie his life. Taking part in a night raid or patrol was frightening, dangerous and often brutal and such events were a more common experience of trench life for the "Poor Bloody Infantry" than "going over the top". Small patrols would routinely slip into no-man's-land at night to check the wire and search for signs of enemy activity. If they ran into German patrols or wiring parties, there might be ferocious clashes often involving loss of life. On the night of 11 August, however, Charlie led out a special twenty-strong patrol to reconnoitre for a trench raid planned for the following night. Higher Command urgently needed to know which enemy troops were serving opposite, so the 12th SWB were ordered to carry out a raid to capture a prisoner. Captain Pritchard was tasked with planning and leading it. There were to be four parties, with Charlie commanding the centre one and two subalterns leading those to his left and right. Behind them was a support party led by an NCO. The three attacking parties were each about

WELSH HEROES OF THE WAR.

Capt. F. L. Hybart, Glamorgan R.E., of 79, Cowbridge-road, Cardiff, wounded.

Capt. C. M. Pritchard, S.W.B., Newport, died of wounds.

Lieut. Reginald P. Thompson, Somerset Light Infantry, of Llanishen, died of wounds.

Lce.-corporal Nick James, R.W.F., of Mardy, awarded the Military Medal.

Pte. Frank Hathway, Munster Fusiliers, of 62, Baldwin-street, Newport, killed in action.

Pte. Tom Thomas, R.W.F., of Pontypridd, killed in action.

Driver William Jones, Royal Engineers, Cymmer, killed in action.

Private Steve Meredith, Welsh Regiment, Caerau, killed by gas.

Pte. Rees Rees, Welsh Regiment, Caerau, died of wounds.

Pte. W. Atkinson, a Gilfach Bargoed soldier, who has fallen in action.

Pt. Michael Egan, Welsh Regiment, of Aberavon, killed in action.

Pte. W. Salter, Welsh Regiment, of 5, Rutland-street, Grangetown, Cardiff, killed in action.

Pte. W. C. Herniman, Welsh Regiment, of 4, Cecilstreet, Broadway, Cardiff, killed in action.

Pte. E. James, Welsh Regiment, of Penarth, killed in action.

Pte. Ben Chivers, Welsh Regiment, of Treherbert, died of wounds.

Private Percy Pennington, Welsh Regiment, of Cwmavon, missing.

Rifleman Ivor G. Jones, City of London Regiment, of 11, St. Fagan's-street, Cardiff, missing.

Report of Charlie's death in action amongst many others: second from left top row.

twelve strong and were armed with rifles and hand grenades. Each member of the smaller support party carried two canvas buckets of grenades.

So at 10.30 p.m. on 12 August 1916, Charlie led his men out of a saphead and each party then moved cautiously to their allocated positions. At midnight, an artillery barrage was laid down to destroy the wire and then draw away the enemy's attention from the raiders. The attackers then rushed the German trenches but they were met with rifle, machine-gun and shell fire. Charlie was immediately wounded in the wrist but he refused to stop for treatment and carried on, encouraging his men in the heart of the battle and leading them into the enemy positions. Arriving at the trench, he jumped in. It must have been a terrifying experience, not knowing what was lying in wait. Scrambling along the trench, he encountered one of the

Chocques Military Cemetery contains over 1,800 burials. [The War Graves Photographic Project]

enemy and, despite already being wounded, he single-handedly disabled him and clambered back out of the trench with his prisoner. In the meantime, the rest of the raiders had been busy causing as much mayhem as possible in the German trenches. The job done, Charlie now ordered his men back but, already weakening from loss of blood, he was wounded again, this time in the right thigh and, ominously, much more seriously. Unable to carry on, he handed over his prisoner to a fellow officer, while another, Lieutenant Francis Enright, struggled with great difficulty to get him to safety. Seeing this, Private Harry Pickett rushed back for a stretcher and returned through the German fire to help to bring Charlie in. Pickett was later deservedly awarded the Military Medal for this gallant and selfless act – clear evidence of the high regard which Charlie's men had for him. Back in the safety of a trench, Charlie was in a state of collapse but just managed to ask, "Have they got the Hun?" When told that they had, he replied, "Well, I have done my bit." After receiving basic first aid, he was stretchered out of the line and taken to No. 1 Casualty Clearing Station at the village of Chocques, a few miles west of the front.

The raid was considered a great success. It was the first time the 40th Division had captured a prisoner and he was found to have several useful documents in his possession. However, this would have been small comfort for the next of kin of the three South Wales Borderers who died in the raid. In addition, twenty other raiders, as well as Charlie, had been wounded. Moreover, retaliation from the Germans cost the battalion a further two killed and eleven wounded. It is hoped that establishing that a Bavarian regiment was in the line opposite proved to be adequate military intelligence worthy of these casualties.

On 14 August 1916, the battalion moved out of the line to the village of Calonne and it was here that the men heard with deep sorrow that Captain Pritchard had succumbed to his wounds earlier that day. The War Diary records, "The Battalion thus loses a very gallant officer and a chivalrous, generous and large minded gentleman." The Colonel wrote that very day to Charlie's widow and sons to express:

> the grief we all feel at the loss of a brave comrade … His death has cast a gloom over the whole battalion … He did much while with us to cheer us up and to keep us from that depression that sometimes is hard to overcome … He led his men with great dash and bravery … The success

The Pritchard family grave, Christchurch Cemetery, Newport.   *[David Hughes]*

of the enterprise was largely due to his gallant leadership and devotion to duty … He was always as brave as a lion.

He added that had he not died he would have been decorated. This was confirmed the following day when, in announcing that Captain Pritchard was to be recommended for mention in despatches, Divisional HQ also reported that the Major-General of the 40th Division would have recommended him for the Distinguished Service Order "but for the death of this gallant officer". The only gallantry award higher than the DSO was the Victoria Cross but only the VC could be awarded posthumously then, so he never received the decoration he deserved. Charlie Pritchard now lies in Chocques Military Cemetery, where many others who died of wounds at the Casualty Clearing Station are buried.

Of the thirty men who took part in the historic Wales v New Zealand encounter in 1905, two lost their lives in the war. The New Zealand captain David Gallaher is still revered in his homeland. His grave in Belgium is regularly visited by players, while the All Blacks and France compete for a trophy which is named in his honour. Given Charlie Pritchard's inspirational story – one of courage, fortitude and sportsmanship – he too deserves to be remembered with equal pride by his countrymen.

Charles Meyrick Pritchard's headstone at Chocques. [The War Graves Photographic Project]

Perhaps the concluding remarks on this very brave Welshman are best left to Townsend Collins, who knew Charlie very well:

The war has swept away many a great and famous Rugby player who was also a good fellow; but among them all was none with a stouter or kinder heart, more beloved, more lamented than Charlie Pritchard.

David Westacott

Born: Cardiff 10 October 1882.
Killed in action: Wieltje 28 August 1917.

Teams: Grange National School; Grange Stars; Cardiff and District; Cardiff; Glamorgan.

Wales: 1 cap, 1906.

As Private David Westacott embarked for France in February 1915, did his mind go back to a sea-voyage he had taken nine years earlier? It must have been hard for him to forget that particular journey for, not only was he then on his way to Belfast to make his debut for Wales, it also happened to be the roughest sea crossing that any Welsh XV had ever experienced.

Whereas the archetypal Welsh forward might be pictured as a valleys collier, there is another important, but often overlooked, category of working-class contribution to the early Welsh game. Certainly, in the Cardiff area around the time of the Great War, it was dock workers, rather than miners, who were the cornerstone of many local teams. And some, like Billy O'Neill, Jack Brown, Jack Powell and Joe Pugsley, became Welsh internationals. Their Cardiff team-mate "Dai" Westacott was another. These were hard men and it was nothing for them to put in a shift at the docks on the morning of a big game.

Born near the docks in Grangetown in 1882, Dai spent most of his life there. After being taught the game at Grange National School, he began his senior career with Grange Stars, a club which emerged in the early 1890s, one of several hundred teams in Cardiff and district at the time. Rugby was never more popular in the town. Nicknamed the "Bricklayers", the Stars rose quickly to the forefront of local rugby, eventually winning the still highly coveted Cardiff and District Mallett Cup – one of the oldest in the

Grangetown War Memorial, on which Dai's surname is spelled incorrectly. [Siân Prescott]

Cardiff and District RU's Mallett Cup, first held in 1893-4. Dai played for Grange Stars when they defeated Mackintosh 7-0 in the 1902-3 final. [Gareth Thomas]

game – at the Arms Park. Press coverage of the 1902-3 final praised the Cardiff and District Rugby Union for producing so many talented players, commenting that several men on both sides were good enough to represent the town's senior club. One of these was Dai Westacott and, sure enough, the season after securing his Mallett Cup gold medal, he was recruited by Cardiff when only twenty.

He quickly became a stalwart of the Cardiff pack, making 120 appearances over seven seasons. By 1904-5, he had become so indispensable that he played in all thirty fixtures that year. A tough and powerful forward, he was renowned for his enormous strength. This was occasionally demonstrated in his post-match party piece when visiting a local pub. His Cardiff team-mate and fellow docker, George Northmore, would pick up a poker from the fire-place and bend it double. He then passed it to Dai who would pull it back straight! Despite being immensely strong, however, he was a surprisingly fast and elusive runner with the ball in his hands. Sewell claimed that he once even managed to score five tries in a county match against Somerset. He certainly caught the eyes of the selectors with an impressive display for Glamorgan in December 1905, though this was against the much sterner opposition of the All Blacks. Glamorgan lost 9-0, but all agreed it was a flattering margin for New Zealand over what was very much a scratch XV. Disappointingly for Dai, two days later he picked up a shoulder injury against London Welsh and so was forced to pull out of the Cardiff team which faced New Zealand a couple of days afterwards. He had played so well for Glamorgan against the tourists that the press feared his withdrawal would seriously weaken Cardiff's chances and they may have been right.

The 1905-6 season was one of the most successful in Cardiff RFC's proud history as they suffered only a single defeat in their thirty-two fixtures. And that came from the All Blacks, who won 10-8, benefitting from a foolhardy

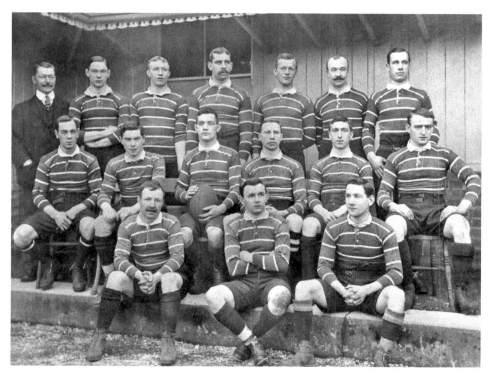

Glamorgan v New Zealand 1905. Back: Dai Westacott is third from right; Dick Thomas is second player from left; Dai "Tarw" Jones stands between them; Middle: Johnny Williams is second from right. [Swansea RFC]

in-goal blunder by Percy Bush. Since it was such a close match, it has to be wondered whether the outcome *might* have been different had Dai been fit to play. Nevertheless, to celebrate what was still an outstanding season, the club presented each of the leading twenty-one players, including Dai, with a commemorative gold watch.

His performances were now regularly coming to the attention of the Welsh rugby establishment. After Glamorgan hammered Somerset 54-5 in January 1906, "Old Stager" suggested it would be a surprise if he were not at least a reserve for the Scotland game: "In the Somerset match his play was brilliant ... he is a consistent hard grafter". Even so, he was still overlooked, but after a fine display in a Cardiff victory over Swansea he was, at last, named in the Welsh XV to meet Ireland. Wales had previously been experimenting with seven forwards and eight backs but the selectors decided to revert to the traditional eight man pack for this game. Dai was one of three new caps in the forwards, all described as "young players in years but each has long experience, and while hard workers in the scrimmage are clever dribblers and opportunistic in open play." One surprising omission though was the unpredictable Percy Bush at outside-half and it may have been a costly one.

Belfast was never an easy place to play but the Welsh team must have viewed the forthcoming match with some optimism. They were, after all, in the middle of a decade of unprecedented success. The team hadn't lost for two years, during which time they had defeated New Zealand, won the 1905 Triple Crown and were two-thirds of the way through another. Ireland had already lost at home to Scotland. Wales only had to beat them to become the first country to win back-to-back Triple Crowns.

So the team left on the Thursday full of confidence. Players and officials from the west caught the train in Swansea and when it reached Cardiff, a saloon and dining car was attached for the Welsh party's use. At Holyhead they embarked for Dublin and, following an overnight stay in the Irish capital, they arrived in Belfast about 3 p.m., allowing time for a training session. It all sounds very straightforward but what the itinerary couldn't allow for was the weather.

It had been raining persistently in Ireland all week and there was heavy sleet and snow in Belfast on the Friday. The conditions on the voyage across the Irish Sea were atrocious. The press reported that "never had Welsh footballers had a worse sea experience." Virtually the whole team went down with acute sea sickness. There can be little doubt that this seriously affected their performance. The training session had to be cut short, while Dicky Owen was so ill, he would not have played had Wales taken a reserve scrum-half.

Wales v Ireland 1906. Back: D Westacott, CM Pritchard, G Travers, W Rees (WRU secretary), T Evans, W Joseph; Middle: J Powell, ET Morgan, J Hodges, EG Nicholls, R Gabe, H Maddock, A Harding: Front: R Owen, HB Winfield, R Gibbs. [WRU]

By match day, however, the weather had turned fine. According to *The Irish Times*, over a thousand Welsh supporters arrived from Liverpool before noon, all wearing the leek: "They were the well-ordered, jolly crowd of enthusiasts they always are, confident of their country's success ... and before the match commenced [they] sang their usual glees". An estimated crowd of 10,000 was the largest to attend a Belfast international so far.

The match result was a disappointing surprise for the Welsh contingent. There was no Triple Crown. Reggie Gibbs was such a failure at outside-half that Hopkin Maddock was moved in from the wing to replace him in the second half. Rhys Gabe had an uncharacteristically poor game and even Gwyn Nicholls seemed demoralised according to the *Manchester Guardian*, while at times Bert Winfield's defence was "far from heroic". But the cause of weakness of the Welsh backs lay with the forwards, who seemed slow and sluggish compared to their opponents. Far superior in the loose, the Irish were much quicker at getting in amongst the opposition backs and disrupting their play. To make matters more embarrassing, Ireland lost one player before half-time and another with ten minutes to go, so they were left with only thirteen men and finished the game with no recognised half-backs.

Against Ireland's three tries and a conversion, Wales did manage two tries and had one fair score disallowed, but Ireland's 11-6 win was a just result. The third Irish try was scored by Basil Maclear, a winger who gave Wales a host of trouble throughout the game.[1] "Old Stager" thought that it was Wales's worst performance in ten years and that Ireland were overwhelmingly the superior team. He did comment that it was impossible to estimate the effect of the sea-sickness, but generously added, "it would be unsporting, if not contemptible" to attribute the defeat to the influence of the dreadful crossing. Wales were soundly beaten.

Whether or not Dai contributed to the deficiencies in the Welsh pack that day, it seems he became associated with the disappointing failure in Belfast and both he and his fellow debutant Jack Powell were never selected again. It is hard to believe that a player of Dai's quality could not normally at least match the Irish. As anyone who has suffered from sea sickness would probably agree, its debilitating effect should surely have been taken into account in making judgements about any of the players. But Welsh rugby has always been a demanding and often unforgiving sport.

However, there was still the club game. Just over two years later, in December 1908, Dai made up for his disappointment in missing Cardiff's match with the All Blacks, by taking part in their crushing 24-8 victory over the touring Australians. The visitors had just become Olympic champions, having defeated the only other entrants, Cornwall, who as English County Champions, had been selected to represent Britain. The scale of Cardiff's success against the Wallabies suggests that it would have been a better idea to have invited the Welsh club to contest the gold medal match.

Even before the Wallabies game started, Cardiff gained the initiative and they never lost it. Australian officials had instructed their players to imitate the All Blacks' haka by performing their own "war dance". The tourists hated it: their "gravest affliction" according to their captain Paddy Moran. As they went through their contrived routine, the Australians' embarrassment must have turned to dismay when the irrepressible Percy Bush faced up to them, theatrically brandishing a Zulu assegai and shield. One wonders what the reaction would be today if a modern Percy Bush attempted something similar during a haka. Anyway, in 1908 it was fair game. First blood to Cardiff.

---

[1] One of the most gifted players to lose his life in the war, Captain Basil Maclear of the 2nd Battalion The Royal Dublin Fusiliers was killed in 1915 near Wieltje during the Second Battle of Ypres.

Cardiff supporters at the Arms Park around Dai Westacott's time. How many of these served in the war?

The Wallabies were overwhelmed that day in one of the most exciting displays of rugby witnessed at the Arms Park. The forwards performed particularly well and outshone their bigger and heavier opponents, especially in the loose. Dai was now a seasoned campaigner and he was at the heart of the Cardiff performance, though he might easily not have finished the game. Early in the second half, the referee spotted the Australian, Albert Burge, kneeing him in the groin as was getting up from a maul. As Dai lay on the ground in agony, Burge was ordered off. Heading towards the pavilion, he was loudly booed by the 30,000 crowd, who recognised him as the player responsible for concussing the Welsh captain Billy Trew in the international a few weeks earlier. Burge had a reputation for dirty play and several of the Wallabies thought that he should not have been picked for the tour. He later maintained that it was not a deliberate foul, claiming that Dai had the ball between his feet when he was getting up and, as he (Burge) tried to kick it, his knee "accidentally" collided with his groin. Burge was the third Australian to be dismissed in Britain and it left an unhappy mark on the tour with accusations of brutal play on the one hand and counter-claims of biased refereeing on the other.

With no substitutes, Dai courageously decided to stay on the field even though, as Cardiff were already 9-3 up and Australia were reduced to fourteen men, he might easily have left with honour. He clearly had been badly hurt and it might reasonably be assumed that he coasted the rest of

INTERNATIONAL KILLED.

D. Westacott.

Private David Westacott, who was a prominent figure in Cardiff and district Rugby Union football, and played regularly for several seasons for the Cardiff Football Club, and also took part in an International game against Ireland at Belfast in 1906, has been killed in France. He served in the Gloucestershire Regiment. In a letter of sympathy to the widow, who lives in Hewell-street, Grangetown, Cardiff, an officer states that death was instantaneous in action, and bears testimony to her husband's efficiency as a soldier and his popularity among his comrades. "He died," writes the officer, "as he lived—a true sportsman." When he enlisted he was employed at the Cardiff Wharf of the Glasgow and Dublin steamers. There are four children.

Report of Dai Westacott's death in action.

the game. That was not so, however. With a few minutes remaining, this tough forward broke away with the ball and made straight for the line. Seeing the Australian defence closing in on him as he neared the goal, he thought better of trying to score himself and passed to Johnny Williams, who sprinted in for Cardiff's fifth and final try. No-one witnessing this electrifying score could possibly have imagined the fate that was lying in wait for both men.

Although Dai was unlucky in his international career, he certainly shone as a club player. This was a period of considerable success for Cardiff RFC. During Dai's seven seasons with the club, only thirty fixtures were lost out of the 221 contested and he played regularly with some of rugby's all-time greats like Gwyn Nicholls, Percy Bush, Bert Winfield and Rhys Gabe. He had the misfortune, however, to become involved in controversy in his last ever appearance for the First XV, against Newport in February 1910. This derby match was always keenly fought and, according to the *Western Mail*, it could sometimes excite more interest than Welsh internationals. But this particular game turned out to be the bitterest and dirtiest confrontation of the 113 so far played between the two clubs. Danny Davies, the Cardiff RFC historian who played for the club throughout the 1920s, claimed that it was responsible for bad feeling which spilled over well into the post-war decade.

The meeting at Rodney Parade was the fourth of the season, and there was a great deal at stake because Newport were still then undefeated. The match, which Cardiff eventually won 9-8, was characterised by a great deal of fouling, kicking, punching and late tackling. In the course of play, the referee sent off Newport's Welsh-born English international Reg Edwards for a foul on Percy Bush. Then he spotted a Newport player being throttled in a maul and, in a clear case of mistaken identity, picked out Dai as the culprit. Dai was dismissed from the field, and later suspended until the following October, though he had decided to retire by then. Not only the *Western Mail*, but also a WRU official, later acknowledged that Dai had suffered a serious injustice. At the time, the WRU's policy when dealing with disciplinary cases was to consider *only* the referee's report and *no* other evidence. Even the opinion of some of the Cardiff players who could have identified the real culprit was ignored. Dai was not allowed to defend himself and there was no right of appeal. It was a sorry and unjust way for such a sterling career with Cardiff to end.

On the other hand, Dai's final appearance at the Arms Park in a charity match, in November 1913, shows the very best side of Welsh rugby. A month earlier, 439 men and boys had been killed at Senghenydd in Britain's worst mining accident. We may rightly baulk at the hideous scale of battlefield casualties during the Great War, but this tragedy is a stark reminder that even in peacetime our mining communities could suffer terrible loss of life. Like most mining villages, Senghenydd had its own keenly supported rugby club. A little over a year before the accident, they had played at the Arms Park in the final of Cardiff and District's Ninian Stuart Cup, which they eventually won after a replay. Many of their supporters had walked the ten miles to Whitchurch where the semi-final had been held, but for the final they chartered a special train to Cardiff. Distressingly, many who had participated in these events were later involved in the explosion. It was only natural, therefore, that the Cardiff club would want to support the Disaster Fund. Dai, together with Johnny Williams and Dick Thomas, turned out for Cardiff Past in their 11 all draw with Cardiff Present.

Despite being thirty-two and a family man with four young children, Dai volunteered early in the war, enlisting in The Gloucestershire Regiment in Cardiff on 15 November 1914. Before leaving, Dai left instructions that if anything happened to him, his Cardiff RFC gold watch should go to his son David, who himself played for Cardiff in later years. In 1972, Dai's grandson Peter Westacott very generously presented the watch to the Cardiff club, where it can be seen in the trophy room to this day.

Only a week before Dai enlisted, the campaign to recruit the Cardiff City Battalion began. Since this unit had a very strong Cardiff RFC contingent, had Dai held back just a few more days he might perhaps have found himself preparing for war in The Welsh Regiment alongside his old team-mates. The Army probably seemed a chance to escape the hard toil and drudgery of dock work for a while, though by this time, any thoughts of "over by Christmas" had long been dispelled.

Dai underwent training at Woolwich and, in a remarkably short time, found himself on his way to France in a draft of twenty NCOs and men, which joined the 1st Battalion The Gloucestershire Regiment of the 1st Division in February 1915. This Regular Army battalion had already suffered many casualties since it went out to France in August 1914, most recently during the unsuccessful German attack at Givenchy on the 25th January. Only two weeks before Dai arrived, another former international, the English forward, Henry Berry, joined the battalion.

Dai only had a couple of days familiarising himself with army routine

CARDIFF FOOTBALL CLUB.

Invincible Inter-Club Record, Season 1905-1906.

A
Reproduction
of the
21 Watches
presented to
the Cardiff
Team.

The Order
was secured
in open
Competition
by

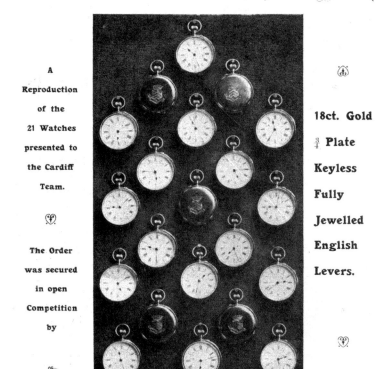

18ct. Gold

¾ Plate

Keyless

Fully

Jewelled

English

Levers.

Messrs. T. W. LONG & Co.,
2, ST. MARY STREET,
CARDIFF.

CUPS, BOWLS, SHIELDS, BADGES,
At Competitive Prices.

The gold watches presented to Cardiff players in 1905-6.

in comparative safety, before the Gloucesters went back up the line at Festubert. His war now began in earnest. The area was relatively quiet at the time but even so conditions were very far from comfortable. There were no trenches as such, just a series of breastworks, while the ground behind the front line was extremely muddy and had few shelters.

On 9 May 1915, the British began an offensive to try to break the German line in the Battle of Aubers Ridge. The 1st Gloucesters had to attack enemy trenches near Richebourg L'Avoué but they were held up by fierce machine-gun and rifle fire which caused heavy losses. They suffered 264 casualties and amongst those killed was Henry Berry. Despite the severity of the fighting, Dai appears to have survived the attack unscathed as he did again when his battalion took part in their next major action, the Battle of Loos in September-October 1915. On 8 October, the 1st Division were holding a line just north-east of Loos, when the Germans launched a major counter-attack. Despite being heavily outnumbered, the 1st Gloucesters halted and then drove back the Germans before they could reach the British trenches.

After about a year's active service involving two major battles, Dai went on a well-deserved home leave. On his return to the Western Front he was transferred to the 14th (Service) Battalion (West of England) The Gloucestershire Regiment, a "New Army" unit which had been raised in Bristol and which went out to France in January 1916. Dai must have stood out in more ways than one as this was a "Bantam" battalion originally recruited from men with a minimum height of five feet three inches (1.6m). Small they may have been, but many were tough miners from the rugby stronghold of the Forest of Dean. As part of the 35th Division, the 14th Gloucesters were one

Tyne Cot Cemetery. The panels of the Memorial to the Missing can be seen in the background.   [Gary Williams]

of the many Kitchener units which took part in the Battle of the Somme. On 23 August 1916, they were in the line just south of Guillemont. During the evening, they were subjected to heavy shellfire for about an hour which caused forty-five casualties. One of these was Dai. Wounded in both legs, he was evacuated from the battlefield and later treated in hospital in Bristol. He then spent eight months with the 3rd (Reserve) Battalion in Kent. Fully recovered from his wounds, he returned to the Western Front for the third and final time in the summer of 1917.

He was then transferred to yet another battalion of The Gloucestershire Regiment, this time to the 2/6th Battalion which was in the 183rd Brigade, 61st (2nd South Midland) Division. This too had been raised in Bristol at the beginning of the war. Unlike the 14th Battalion, it was a Territorial Force unit, though by late 1917, the distinction between Regular, Territorial and New

Grangetown War Memorial in Grange Gardens, near Dai's home in Hewell Street. [Siân Prescott]

Army units had become blurred. In August 1917, the 2/6th were engaged in the bitter slog of the Third Battle of Ypres. On 27 August they went into the front line north-east of Ypres near Wieltje – very close to the spot where Dai's old Irish adversary, Basil Maclear, had died two years earlier – to provide a welcome relief for a sister battalion in the 183rd Brigade which had just taken part in an unsuccessful attack.

The 2/6th Battalion War Diary noted that the artillery was active that particular day. But for the next, 28 August 1917, it merely recorded laconically "artillery quieter on both sides all day". There was no mention of casualties. But "quieter" doesn't mean "quiet". After bravely suffering so much hardship and surviving several major battles, Private David Westacott was killed in a support trench that day by a random shell. As was almost invariably the practice at the time, his death was reported as "instantaneous". He was buried the following day but, as often happened, the location of his grave was subsequently lost. He is now commemorated, not far from where he was killed, on the Tyne Cot Memorial to the Missing near Zonnebeke. This bears the names of nearly 35,000 who died in the Ypres Salient after 16 August 1917 and whose graves are unknown.

But he is also commemorated much nearer home. Very close to where he lived in Hewell Street, on a part of Grange Gardens which he must have passed frequently on his way to the Arms Park, there now stands a war memorial which lists the names of all the men of Grangetown who, like Dai Westacott, courageously served their country but did not return home to their loved ones after the war.

The Gloucestershire Regiment panel, Tyne Cot Memorial.   [britishcemeteries.webs.com]

Richard Thomas

Born: Ferndale 14 October 1883.
Killed in action: Mametz Wood 7 July 1916.

Teams: Ferndale; Penygraig; Cardiff; Mountain Ash; Llwynypia; Bridgend; Glamorgan Police; Glamorgan League; Glamorgan.

Wales: 4 caps, 1906-1909.

William Davies of the 11th (Service) Battalion (2nd Gwent) The South Wales Borderers was one of the last survivors of the Welsh Division's opening attack on Mametz Wood on 7 July 1916. Seventy-one years later, he gave an interview to the BBC about the harrowing events of that blood-soaked day, during which he recalled witnessing the death of one comrade in particular:

> I remember one man, he was an old rugby international, Company Sergeant Major Dick Thomas from Mountain Ash ... he was a big huge man, lying down in front of me ... and he got up on his knee and two hands, you know, knees on the ground ... (then he) went down ... head down to the ground ... killed just like that ... just in front of me ... and I hid behind him all day.

It is not surprising that William Davies recognised "Dick" Thomas because he had been very well-known in Welsh rugby circles and beyond. The English journalist EHD Sewell wrote of him:

> Wales has had some fairly hefty and tough men in her pack from time to time. Burly and hard bitten sons of the hills most of them, caring little or nothing for physical hurt whether to self or opponent, and one of

the toughest and the fairest was "Dick" Thomas who, as one of his friends has written to me, "could always take a knock without moving a hair; this served him as well in the police force as on the football field."

Sewell also quoted the comments of the WRU official, T. D. Schofield of Bridgend, who knew Dick well:

He was ... the life and soul of any team. Gentle by no means, he nevertheless never failed to play the game properly. He would take and give hard knocks. A hard working scrimager [sic], he was no less prominent in the open. He was a fearless tackler and had the happy knack of adapting himself to any circumstances of emergency.

I am betraying no secret when I say that he was a warm favourite with all members of the Welsh Rugby Union Selection Committee, and it was only an attack of appendicitis which prevented his inclusion in the Welsh International team on many more occasions ... He was a man beloved by both players and spectators, and his loss to the Rugger Code in Wales is as irreparable as it is deplored. He died as he had always lived, a great hero.

Sergeant Richard Thomas, of Bridgend, killed in action. He was in the Welsh Regiment.

Report of Dick Thomas's death.

Though he is sometimes referred to as "Edward John" Richard Thomas, his forename is invariably "Richard" or "Dick" in rugby, police and military records and in press reports. He was born in Ferndale, Rhondda in 1883[1], and spent the early years of his working life underground as a collier. His first experience of senior rugby was with his local club Ferndale. However, he switched to the Glamorgan League club Penygraig and very quickly made his mark there. In 1904-5, while still a Penygraig player, he won the first of his twenty county caps and he was also selected reserve forward for Wales who won the Triple Crown that season. After the England match, "Forward" even argued that he should be brought in to strengthen the

---

1   However, his police records indicate his year of birth as 1881.

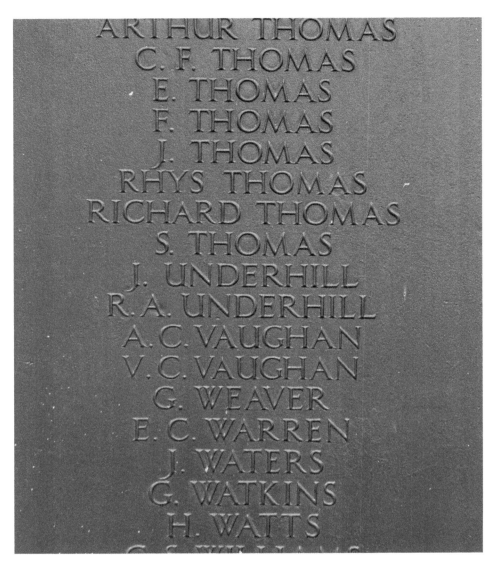

Bridgend War Memorial. [Siân Prescott]

Welsh team. It seems that the Cardiff club were showing an interest too for, over the Christmas period, he had a couple of games for their reserves and then played for the First XV against Moseley. Helping Cardiff to a six-try win, Dick was described as the best forward on the field. Selected for the following match at Leicester, a glittering career with the Blue and Blacks was now a real possibility. However, it was not to be. Only a few weeks earlier, Dick had joined the Glamorgan Constabulary and it was no

One of Dick's many appearances for Glamorgan in 1910. He is in the back row second from left. [Swansea RFC]

doubt this which prevented him from joining Cardiff on a permanent basis. Posted to the Aberdare Division, he saw out the season with Penygraig but in the following summer he transferred to Mountain Ash, with whom he was to win all his four Welsh caps. Founded in 1875, Mountain Ash have always been at or very near the top of the Welsh club game and they were a powerful team when Dick joined them. Always strong contenders in the Glamorgan League from its inception in 1894-5, they were champions three times before the Great War and Dick was a member of their 1908-9 Championship winning side.

From 1905 onwards, Dick also figured regularly in the Glamorgan Police XV. They could usually draw on some fine players, including several internationals but, though their packs were invariably strong, they sometimes lacked quality backs. It is a measure of Dick's all-round footballing skills that, on many occasions, he helped out at half back or three-quarter for the County Police. In the days before substitutes, an injury to a back inevitably meant that a forward would have to be moved out, so a player with Dick's footballing skills and experience was a real bonus for any team. He remained a stalwart of the Police team right up to 1914 and played in their last pre-war game against, appropriately enough, his first club, Ferndale. Useful with his fists, he was also the Glamorgan Police heavyweight boxing champion three times and in 1909 won an assault-at-arms competition, open to members of the Glamorgan and Monmouthshire forces.

Besides his appearances for Penygraig and Mountain Ash in the Glamorgan League, Dick also came to the attention of the Welsh selectors in his frequent outings for the Police and for Glamorgan County. In December 1905, he was a member of the Glamorgan team which gave the All Blacks such a scare just five days after the international. Dick's performance was described by one Welsh selector as "head and shoulders above any other forward on the field."

The following October, he was again impressive in another close match for the County, this time against the Springboks who won 6-3. This performance led to his first game in the Welsh jersey against South Africa in December 1906. Wales were expected to win. They hadn't lost at Swansea for eleven years; it was only a year since the defeat of New Zealand; and Dick was joining Charlie Pritchard and five other forwards who played in that triumph. Yet against all expectations, the Welsh pack were trounced and, with half-backs Dicky Owen and Percy Bush combining poorly, the three-quarters had few attacking opportunities. Even the Springboks were surprised at the ease of their 11-0 triumph. Reuter reported that "the victory created immense enthusiasm throughout South Africa. Crowds thronged outside the newspaper offices in all the towns and villages awaiting the progress of the game. The result was received with extraordinary gratification and surprise. Cheering crowds marched through the streets for hours afterwards." This is a measure of just how highly regarded Wales were at this time.

Dick contracted appendicitis soon after – a potentially life-threatening condition then – and this kept him out of rugby until the following season. He eventually returned to the Welsh team in March 1908 for the first ever meeting with France. Even though the game had been scheduled for a Monday, the novelty of the fixture meant that 15,000 supporters still turned up at the Arms Park. This time Dick's experience of international rugby proved to be a far more enjoyable one as Wales attacked strongly from the outset and scored nine tries in a 36-4 victory. The French showed some good individual skills but were completely lacking in combination. In defence, they were regularly outfoxed by Welsh specialities like the reverse pass and the miss pass. The Toulouse scrum-half, Alfred Mayssonnié, however, was praised for his accurate kicking. Sadly he was to become rugby's first wartime fatality when he was killed on 6 September 1914. Two others in that French XV, Gaston Lane and Pierre Guillemin, also lost their lives in the war.

After his "sterling play" against France, Dick kept his place for the historic final match in Belfast in March 1908. The game was stalled at 5 all with

Wales v Ireland 1908. This was the first ever international team to win a Grand Slam. Back: AJ Webb, G Hayward, R Thomas, TH Evans, W. O'Neill, W Dowell; Middle: G Travers, R Gibbs, W Trew, HB Winfield, R Gabe, JL Williams, J Watts; Front: R Jones, R Owen. [WRU]

ten minutes to go when the Welsh backs struck, scoring two spectacular tries in three minutes, one by Johnny Williams. In winning 11-5, Wales not only took their fifth Triple Crown, they also achieved the first ever Grand Slam. According to "Old Stager", Dick was the best forward on the field and merited "special praise for his all-round work." So he thought it inexplicable when Dick was over-looked for the Australian international the following December, especially after he had played so well for Glamorgan against the tourists. It is likely that he would have been selected for the following match against England in January 1909, but for an "ugly" incident – probably a retaliatory swinging fist – which occurred during the Glamorgan League's 11-3 defeat at the hands of the Wallabies in Pontypridd. This was another game, incidentally, in which he stood out amongst his peers. The press were rather coy about what happened but, when the team for England was announced, "Old Stager" had this to say:

> R. Thomas, who played so brilliantly in Ireland last season, would probably have regained his place in the team but for the prejudice against him which has gained in force since a regrettable incident in the Glamorgan League game against The Wallabies.

Reading between the lines, we can speculate as to what the cause of the "prejudice" was. We know he had a reputation for taking and giving hard knocks. One opponent once said of him, "the Monmouthshire League team would sooner face any man than Dick Thomas" but "Old Stager" was clearly a fan. Good sense seems to have prevailed eventually and he was brought back to bring more steel to the pack against Scotland in February 1909. Even so, the forwards still struggled, but Wales went on to win 5-3. Dick was named in the team for France but dropped out after being taken ill and he also missed the Irish game. Both ended in victory. The Scottish match was Dick's last international but he could look back with great pride in having helped Wales to two successive Triple Crowns and Grand Slams.

During periods of serious unrest in the coalfield, Dick was commended several times for actions above the call of duty. When the "Rhondda Riots" of 1910-11 broke out, he spent some time stationed in Rhondda, yet despite the confrontations between police and strikers, he was still invited to turn out occasionally for local clubs like Llwynypia and Ferndale, which must reveal something about his standing in the community.

After six seasons with Mountain Ash, Dick was posted to Bridgend in September 1911. There he joined the town club and continued to impress. When playing for the Whites in the Welsh trial he was "as fast and clever as ever" and his form was still good enough, according to "Old Stager", for a return to the Welsh team. As it was, he chosen as travelling reserve to Ireland. The following season, despite now being nearly thirty, he was offered terms to turn professional, probably not for the first time. Remarkably, right up to 1914 the local press continued to comment regularly on how well he was playing for Bridgend and the Glamorgan Police.

The distinctive collar badge worn by Other Ranks in the Cardiff City Battalion. [Siân Prescott]

With the coming of war, Dick was one of a strong contingent of Glamorgan policemen who joined the 16th (Service)

Battalion (Cardiff City) The Welsh Regiment. According to the CO, Lieutenant Colonel Frank Gaskell, the police made a vital contribution to the newly formed battalion: "A great number of constables of the Glamorgan Constabulary joined the Battalion in the early days of December and these trained men ... gave backbone to the new establishment."

One of Dick's police colleagues was Fred Smith, twice vice-captain of Cardiff who had come close to being capped at forward by Wales. They had played together many times for Bridgend, Glamorgan Police and the Glamorgan County XV. Fred had served in the South African War and joined the 16th Welsh as a lieutenant in December 1914. By April 1915, he had been promoted to major and was second in command of the battalion. No doubt Dick's friendship with Fred encouraged him to enlist in the City Battalion.

The 16th Welsh were raised in Cardiff during a vigorous eight-week recruiting campaign beginning in November 1914. The first recruits went into billets in Porthcawl but, with the rest of the Welsh Division concentrating in north Wales, the City Battalion moved to Colwyn Bay on 30 December. Because of his police commitments, Dick was unable to enlist until 16 January 1915, so it was in north Wales that he first joined the battalion as

The Commanding Officer of the Cardiff City Battalion, Fred Smith, with the ball, was captain for the day when Cardiff defeated Stade Bordelais 21-5 in France in 1909.

a private. Besides Fred Smith, there were many familiar rugby comrades to welcome him there, including Johnny Williams. His general demeanour and bearing, his leadership skills and his experience in handling men in all kinds of situations meant that Dick was quickly recognised as ideal NCO material and so, within two months, he had been promoted to company sergeant major. In late August, the battalion moved to the Hazeley Down camp near Winchester for final preparation for the Western Front. Like other Kitchener units, throughout their period of training, the City Battalion had to cope with a serious lack of equipment of all kinds, especially weapons, and it was only after arriving at Hazeley that Dick and his men were able to begin practising with the Lee-Enfield rifles they would soon be using in combat. Then came a brief return to Cardiff where they marched through the city and were inspected by the Lord Mayor at the Arms Park. There have been many emotional scenes at the famous old ground over the years, but it is doubtful if it has ever witnessed a more moving one than that day, as the officers and men of the 16th Welsh took their farewell of their loved ones. A couple of days later on 4 December 1915, the City Battalion, as part of the 115th Brigade, 38th (Welsh) Division, were on their way to the battlefields of France. Within seven months, around half of the thousand men who paraded so proudly at the Arms Park had been killed or wounded, or were missing.

The 38th Division spent December 1915 undergoing an apprenticeship in trench warfare before taking over part of the line north of Loos and they remained in the Neuve Chapelle, Festubert and Givenchy area for the next six months. This sector was largely quiet at the time, though the conditions were extremely wet and miserable in places. There were no major attacks but several battalions, including the 16th, gained experience in trench raiding. It may have been "quiet" but there was still a steady toll of casualties, amongst whom was Lieutenant Colonel Gaskell who was killed by a sniper in May. As a consequence, Fred Smith was promoted to Lieutenant Colonel and took over command of the battalion. On 11 June, the Division was withdrawn from the line and began the long trek south to the Somme. During the evening of the horrendous opening day of the Battle of the Somme, they began moving up towards the forward area and on 5 July the weary troops of the 38th (Welsh) Division took over part of the front just below Mametz Wood, a name that was soon to become, sadly, all too familiar in households across Wales.

A two-pronged approach to the capture of the wood was planned for 7 July, with the 38th (Welsh) Division attacking the wood from the east, supported by the 17th (Northern) Division from the south-west. The 115th Brigade was tasked with carrying out the Welsh Division's first major attack and the City Battalion were selected to lead it. Their target was a projection of the wood called the "Hammerhead" and the battalion would make its attack at 8.30 a.m. from a 500 yard start line between Caterpillar Wood and Marlborough Wood, just to the right of where the 38th Division dragon memorial stands today. This would require the troops to advance down a slope, cross "Death Valley" and then charge up to and into the wood. It was a supremely difficult enough task in itself but one made far more dangerous because it would take place at right angles to the German second line and two forward copses where the enemy were well dug in. Lieutenant Colonel Smith immediately expressed concern that his right flank would be perilously exposed to enfilade fire from Flatiron Copse, which was less than 200 yards away. His request to

The 38th (Welsh) Division Memorial at Mametz Wood was raised by the South Wales Branch of the Western Front Association in 1987. The dragon was sculpted by David Petersen. [Gary Williams]

cross the open land in front of the Hammerhead before dawn was rejected: the start-time had to remain at 8.30 to synchronise with the 17th Division. Later, at short notice, it was decided to add a second battalion to the attack and so the 11th South Wales Borderers were ordered to take up the left flank, with the City battalion bunched on the dangerously exposed right.

The artillery was supposed to deal with the Germans dug in at the edge of the wood and in Flatiron Copse and Sabot Copse on the flank. In addition, a smoke screen was to be laid down to provide cover. As soon as the artillery bombardment lifted, the leading waves of the two battalions came over the crest of a rise, which up to now had protected them, and they advanced down the slope towards the menacing wood. Fatefully, there was no smoke cover – it never materialised – and all too quickly it became clear that the artillery had not neutralised the enemy either. The attackers were immediately caught by devastating machine-gun fire both from the wood and from the two copses and the German second line on the right flank. It soon became a bullet-swept killing zone. Successive waves were caught in the withering frontal and enfilade fire as they came over the crest. Based on William Davies's recollections, it is likely that Dick was on the left of the City Battalion near the centre of the attack when he was shot. Other reports imply that this happened early on, suggesting that he may have been leading his men in one of the first waves.

Not surprisingly, the ill-conceived attack came to a standstill and, about 250 yards from the wood, the survivors desperately took what cover they could find. Wyn Griffith was an eyewitness to these events and he later described the terrifying scene in his classic account "Up to Mametz":

> Every attempt to move near the wood was met by a burst of frontal and enfilade machine-gun fire ... our men were burrowing into the ground with their entrenching tools, seeking whatever cover they might make ... Wounded men were crawling back ... men were crawling forward with ammunition. No attack could succeed over such ground as this, swept from front and side by machine guns at short range.

Later in the day, the 10th (Service) Battalion (1st Gwent) The South Wales Borderers launched an attack in support but this too was brought to a halt. Eventually, in the early evening, the survivors of the three battalions were withdrawn. Being more exposed from the right flank, the 16th Welsh had been most severely hit, suffering nearly 300 casualties, with around 140 killed or mortally wounded, amongst whom was Johnny Williams. The 38th Division renewed the attack on a larger scale on 10 July from a position further south and to the left of the memorial and, with enormous courage, after days of desperately bitter fighting, they drove the Germans out of all but a small strip of the wood by 12 July. It was for his courage in capturing a machine-gun here that the Pontypridd and Wales forward, Lieutenant Frank Hawkins of the 14th (Service) Battalion (Swansea) The Welsh Regiment was awarded the Military Cross. The capture of the largest wood on the Somme in such a short time was a magnificent military achievement but it cost the Welsh Division 4,000 casualties.

The day after the City Battalion's attack, Glamorgan Policeman RSM John Thomas wrote to his wife that Dick Thomas had been one of the first to be killed, adding: "We are very much upset over the loss of Dick. He used to keep the lot of us alive with his jokes." One of the saddest duties of an officer during the war was writing to the next of kin of the men who had died under his command. It must have been particularly heart-wrenching though for Fred Smith when he had to write to the widow and two children

Bridgend War Memorial. *[Siân Prescott]*

of his old team-mate and colleague in Bridgend: "I am deeply grieved to tell you ... my old friend Dick was killed while attacking a wood. He died at once and did not suffer. I had already recommended him for an MC for his gallantry and splendid example to his men." Like Charlie Pritchard, however, Dick never received a decoration because the Military Cross could not then be awarded posthumously.

As with a hundred other City Battalion men who died in the attack, Dick Thomas's body was never identified, although he is possibly buried as an "Unknown" in Flatiron Copse Cemetery where many of the fallen of the 38th Division now lie. He is, however, commemorated by the Commonwealth War Graves Commission on the Thiepval Memorial to the Missing of the Somme. In 2006, he and Johnny Williams were the subject of an ITV Wales documentary, "The First Fifteen"; while in the church in Mametz village, above a memorial plaque to the 38th (Welsh) Division, a framed photograph of Dick was placed in his remembrance by a party from St. Martin's School, Caerphilly in 2007. "Missing" perhaps, but not forgotten.

Thiepval Memorial.   [Gwyn Prescott]

John Lewis Williams

Born: Whitchurch 3 January 1882.
Died of wounds: Corbie 12 July 1916.

Teams: Whitchurch; Newport; Cardiff; London Welsh; Glamorgan; Great Britain (Anglo-Welsh) 1908.

Wales: 17 caps, 1906-1911.

Even though over 130 internationals died in the First World War, only a select few are widely known. While the stories of men like Ronald Poulton, Edgar Mobbs and David Gallaher are undeniably worth retelling, there are many others whose achievements deserve similar recognition. One such is John Lewis Williams, the flying left wing who was certainly one of finest players of all those who died in the war. According to the *South Wales Daily News*, he was "a great footballer; always a trier and a universal favourite with the crowd." EHD Sewell wrote of his "brilliant career" and praised him for his "sure tackling, fielding and kicking, combined with a deceptive turn of speed and, above all, a capital swerve".

His record speaks for itself:

- seventeen Welsh caps between 1906 and 1911, during which time he was on the losing side only twice;
- three Grand Slams/Triple Crowns;
- second highest ever try average for Wales, with seventeen tries in seventeen matches;
- two British Test appearances in New Zealand 1908, when he was the leading try scorer;
- three hundred games in top flight rugby;
- twelve seasons of elite club rugby, including Cardiff's comprehensive victories over South Africa and Australia; and

- Cardiff try record for forty years.

Born in Whitchurch, then a village just outside Cardiff, his father was a farmer and overseer of the poor. "Johnny" (or Johnnie – the spelling varies) attended Cowbridge Grammar School, which had pioneered rugby in Wales during the 1870s. He was not introduced to the

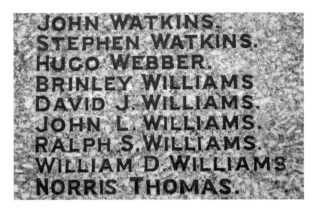

Whitchurch War Memorial. *[Siân Prescott]*

game there though. By his time, Cowbridge had switched – for a period – to

Whitchurch War Memorial. *[Siân Prescott]*

soccer, so it was for the round ball version of football that he won his school colours.

Despite his talent for soccer, however, his ambition was to emulate his sporting heroes at the Arms Park, so he took up rugby with his local club. Established in 1885, Whitchurch were an ambitious junior team and had recently developed a new enclosed ground and stand and had also just become members of the WRU. He made an immediate impact there and it wasn't long before more senior clubs began taking an interest in the promising young three-quarter. However, it wasn't Cardiff who recruited him, but their arch rivals Newport, who gratefully snapped him up after he had stood out in a match against their Reserves.

He made his debut at Rodney Parade in September 1899. It

must have been daunting for a mere seventeen year-old to play with the likes of George Boots, Jehoida Hodges and Llewellyn Lloyd, but he overcame any nervousness and managed to cross for a try in a comfortable win over Penarth. Also in the Newport XV that day was Lou Phillips, and for the next season and a half, until Lou suffered his career-ending injury, the two men, who were both destined to die in France, remained team-mates.

Newport Athletic Club War Memorial. [Siân Prescott]

Johnny stayed at Newport for four seasons, playing in forty-nine fixtures, at first mainly as a centre but eventually settling on the left wing. In 1903-4, however, he decided to switch to his home-town club for whom he went on to play 199 times. Also in his first season with Cardiff that year was Rhys Gabe, one of the greatest centres ever to come out of Wales and with whom Johnny was to form a dazzling left centre/wing partnership – "the very acme of polished cleverness in all they did" in the opinion of the *Western Mail*.

Over the next two years, Johnny worked hard on his speed and on developing his swerve and by the autumn of 1905 he was being described

Cardiff RFC 1910-11. Johnny is seated third row second from right. JMC "Clem" Lewis who served with him in the 16th Welsh is front row left.

as a "wing of tip-top class". He was rewarded with selection for that season's Welsh trial and then for Glamorgan against the All Blacks, when he showed great determination in his tackling, in a narrow defeat in which the scratch county side competed very creditably. Five days later, Johnny was facing New Zealand again in Cardiff's heart-breaking 10-8 defeat. A pulsating game which the Blue and Blacks could have won had it not been for the careless mistake by Percy Bush, this was Cardiff's only reverse during 1905-6. With a prolific thirty-five tries, Johnny was responsible for almost half of Cardiff's total that season.

A year later in December 1906, Johnny's rise to prominence continued when he was listed as a reserve for the South African international. However, not everyone thought this was good enough. In the *Western Mail*, "Forward" argued that he had been so consistently impressive all season he deserved to be in the XV. In Glamorgan's 24-3 demolition of Monmouthshire, he was "by far and away the best wing on the field and his brilliant dashes impressed everybody". But then Billy Trew pulled out, so Johnny was in the team after all and, despite the shockingly disappointing Welsh display, he justified his selection and was one of the few Welshmen to receive praise from the press.

Within three weeks, however, an opportunity arose to make amends for this disastrous defeat. The Springboks' last fixture in Britain was with Cardiff. According to "Forward", that day, "Wales redeemed her reputation" when the club "achieved one of the greatest triumphs in the whole history of Welsh football". The conditions were awful. The pitch was a sea of mud and a strong wind was blowing but Cardiff still managed a wonderful display of running rugby to overwhelm South Africa by 17 points to nil. Johnny contributed to the Cardiff total and he never scored a better try. Given the ball by Rhys Gabe who had broken upfield, Johnny only had the full-back to beat. Arthur Marsberg was "a holy terror to get by" and rarely missed a tackle, but "Johnny Bach" artfully side-stepped him and sped away for an exhilarating score. Graciously, Marsberg then ran over and shook his hand to acknowledge he had got the better of him. It was a stunning victory and indisputably one of Cardiff's finest ever.

Johnny maintained this form in his next international, crossing for two tries – one of which "raised the roof" – as Wales ran rings round England at Swansea to win 22-0. However, despite fearless defensive work by the three-quarters and especially by Johnny, a 6-3 defeat followed in Edinburgh, though "Forward" was convinced that the Scottish touch-judge had unfairly disallowed a Reggie Gibbs try. This was only the third of Johnny's seventeen internationals but, remarkably, he never again tasted defeat for Wales. The topsy-turvy 1906-7 season ended on a high note with the 29-0 destruction of Ireland at Cardiff. In collecting three of the six Welsh tries, Johnny never looked sharper and he was now even being compared favourably with Teddy Morgan, scorer of the winning try against New Zealand. A few weeks later, Johnny bagged five tries in Cardiff's 38-0 win over the Barbarians.

He next appeared for Wales in the fog-bound match in Bristol in January 1908 when England were despatched 28-18. "Old Stager" put the victory down to the Welsh XV's superior combination and greater individual skills. He also claimed he had taken pleasure in the English performance, but rather marred the compliment when he added somewhat patronisingly, "it was very gratifying to Welshmen to see the improvement in the attacking power of England." How "Old Stager" managed to see *anything* though is open to question. Johnny told the press that the fog spoiled the game. It must have been a nightmare for the winger: "At times we did not know whether we were attacking or defending or which man had the ball".

A week later, Lloyd George was a guest at the Arms Park for Cardiff's match with Blackheath. Happily that day was fog free so everyone was able to see him kick off. The home side won easily and Johnny impressed the future wartime Prime Minister with one of Cardiff's five tries. Ever the politician, he later gave his impressions of the match: "It is a most extraordinary game. I never saw it before today and I must say I think it is more exciting than politics".

In Johnny's sixth consecutive international, Wales were a little lucky to win 6-5 against Scotland at Swansea, where they certainly missed the injured Charlie Pritchard. A perfectly timed pass from Rhys Gabe, enabled Johnny to score a "glorious" winning try although "Forward" thought he wasn't quite showing the class of the previous season. The selectors appear to have agreed because he was dropped for the French match and Teddy Morgan was enticed out of retirement to replace him. However, Johnny was restored to the left wing for the crucial game in March

The future wartime Prime Minister discovers that rugby is more exciting than politics at the Arms Park.

1908 in Belfast, where he demonstrated that he had recovered his old sharpness. Even though carrying a shoulder injury, he proved to be one of the day's successes. "Forward" was particularly pleased to see him doing so well again: "His two tries were beautifully got ... on each occasion he had to beat two or three men." Drawing 5-5 with ten minutes left, Wales went ahead with a Reggie Gibbs try. Then Johnny made the game safe when, after a breath-taking round of passing, he finished off a movement "that sent the whole crowd into raptures". Wales won the match 11-5 and with it a fifth Triple Crown and a first Grand Slam.

A week earlier, it had been announced that Johnny had been selected for the British tour of New Zealand and Australia later that summer. With Ireland and Scotland refusing to participate, this was an Anglo-Welsh team, sometimes referred to in the antipodean press as such but more generally as Britain or even occasionally, and irritatingly for the Welsh contingent, as "the English". As with all previous British tours, the twenty-eight man team was not fully representative and Johnny was one of only eleven who had previously been capped.

It was not a successful tour. Of the twenty-six fixtures, nine were lost, as was the Test series with New Zealand. Johnny played regularly throughout, missing only six games in all. The "greyhound of the team" ended the tour as top try scorer with twelve. The tourists were heavily defeated 32-5 in the first Test when the New Zealand forwards completely dominated the visitors' pack, so it was a surprise when the second Test ended in a 3-3 draw. In dreadfully muddy conditions, this time the British forwards subdued the All Blacks and, with a try to a penalty goal, the tourists were unlucky not to win. In both matches, however, Johnny was given few chances to use his speed and exploit his scoring skills. Injury ruled him out of the third Test, a 29-0 drubbing which restored the true balance of the sides. Johnny was the only participant in this Test series to lose his life in the war.

There were no Tests on the Australian leg of the tour, though Johnny faced the Wallabies four months later, in the international at Cardiff. There were worries that he might not be match fit, having only started playing again a few weeks earlier, but he dispelled any such concerns and was superb in the 9-6 victory. Wales went on to retain the Triple Crown and Grand Slam and, like Phil Waller, Johnny took part in all five of the 1908-9 internationals, scoring once against England and twice against France. He was also one of five Cardiff men to complete a hat-trick of club appearances against the major tourists when he took the field for the Blue and Blacks against the Wallabies. The visitors went down to their heaviest defeat of the tour losing 24-8 and two of Cardiff's five tries were obtained by Johnny, the first from a Reggie Gibbs cross-kick and the second after receiving the ball from Dai Westacott who had dramatically broken away in possession.

All players suffer from a loss of form at some stage and this happened to Johnny during the early part of 1909-10. Perhaps the responsibility of captaining Cardiff initially weighed heavily on him. He was not at his best in the trial and then lost his place in the Welsh team. However, reinstated for the final match in Dublin, he fully vindicated this decision with his second hat-trick for Wales. According to *The Times*, Johnny was the best of the Welsh backs, while "Forward" reported that he "was right on top of his form and his cleverness in beating three or four Irishmen ... before he scored his three tries was really splendid." Each of his tries was the culmination of an exhibition of passing and Wales registered a handsome and thoroughly entertaining 19-3 victory.

The 1910-11 season was Johnny's last in a Welsh jersey and it proved to be yet another memorable one, as Wales went on to record a sixth Triple Crown in eleven years and seventh overall. This time, though, England provided stiffer opposition. "Old Stager" thought that while Wales merited their 15-11 win at Swansea, they were just an average Welsh side which had been severely tested. Johnny had a quiet first half and was beaten several times by his opposite wing Alan Roberts who got the opening try.

Wales v Scotland 1911. Back: G Travers, AJ Webb, Rees Thomas, TH Evans, J Birch, A Coldrick; Middle: J Pugsley, W Spiller, R Gibbs, W Trew, L Dyke, JL Williams, DJ Thomas; Front: R Owen, F Birt. [WRU]

But he made amends in the second half with some wonderful attacking play which delighted the home crowd. However, while the England game was a tight affair, the victory in Scotland proved to be one of the most exceptional feats ever achieved by Wales away from home. With eight tries racked up (only two of which were converted!) and a drop goal, it was a 32-10 rout and a record defeat for Scotland. The Edinburgh press criticised the Scottish backs for being "hopelessly outclassed" by the all-Cardiff three-quarter line which "combined like a machine." *The Times* reported that the Welsh backs "gave a most brilliant display, their passing being a delight to watch." Seven of the Welsh tries were obtained by the three-quarters, two of them by Johnny, who missed a third by inches. So many Welsh supporters had travelled north, that "Forward" claimed they virtually besieged Princes Street, where "it was only by chance that one would meet a Scotsman."

Then followed what "Old Stager" anticipated would be a "pleasant outing to Paris", something no reporter could write again without irony. However, a gutsy French performance convinced him that they were making rapid strides and he warned that in future they "must be taken seriously". Buoyed by France's historic 16-15 win over Scotland, a record 15,000 crowd watched the home side hold Wales to a scoreless first half. Only later did their defence give way, allowing Wales to score three converted tries, one by Johnny – his last in an international – when he pounced on a mistake by the French full-back. On this occasion, Johnny had been honoured with the Welsh captaincy, a fitting gesture since, as a partner in a Cardiff coal-exporting business, he was a fluent French speaker. One prized memento he brought home was the match ball which one day would return again to France but under unusual circumstances.

Johnny retired at the end of 1910-11. In five of his eight seasons with Cardiff he had been the leading try scorer, while his final tally of 150 remained a club record for forty years until eventually surpassed by Bleddyn Williams. However, his final international appearance against Ireland was such a forward-dominated game that he had few opportunities to add to his seventeen Welsh tries.[1] Even so, it was a very satisfying way to end a career of so many highlights. The 1911 Triple Crown showdown attracted a level of interest which even a seasoned international like Johnny had not previously encountered. Cardiff had never witnessed such scenes. Even the attendance for the visit of New Zealand was exceeded, as over 50,000 managed to squeeze into a sweltering Arms Park. Many scaled the walls while others rushed the gates and there were several serious accidents. "Forward"

---

1 Johnny's try rate for Wales of seventeen from seventeen matches is second only to that of Reggie Gibbs, who recorded seventeen in sixteen internationals.

The all-Cardiff three-quarter line-up which played against Ireland at the Arms Park in the Triple Crown decider in 1911. From left: Reggie Gibbs, Billy Spiller, Louis Dyke and Johnny Williams.

noted the unprecedented number of "photographers and cinematographic operators" present. A final score-line of 16-0 gave Wales a fifth consecutive win over Ireland and it meant they had lost only once in eighteen matches. The Triple Crown returned to Wales. Who amongst that vast crowd could have guessed that it would be another thirty-nine years before it came back? But that long wait only reinforces what a truly extraordinary period the first "Golden Era" had been. But now it was over.

It has previously been noted that Johnny returned to the Arms Park with Dai Westacott and Dick Thomas in November 1913 to play in a charity match in aid of the Senghenydd Disaster Fund. However, he would be back there two years later for a very different reason. Only seven weeks after war was declared, Johnny enlisted in Cardiff as a private in the 20th (Service) Battalion The Royal Fusiliers, the same battalion in which Lou Phillips served. Shortly afterwards, he was transferred to the 21st (Service) Battalion (4th Public Schools) The Royal Fusiliers and began training with them at Ashtead, Surrey. There he found himself in a platoon capable of turning out an all-international three-quarter line, with Welsh internationals

Hopkin Maddock and Willie Watts and the English winger Alan Roberts, who had outpaced Johnny for his try against Wales in 1911. Unlike Lou Phillips, however, Johnny decided to apply for a commission and there was one unit in particular in which he was keen to serve.

In late November 1914, the Lord Mayor of Cardiff launched an intensive campaign to raise a battalion of The Welsh Regiment bearing the name of the city. The war was now sixteen weeks old and the so-called "First Rush" of recruits had subsided. Volunteers were still coming in but at a much slower rate, so it was no longer so easy to raise a thousand-strong battalion as it had been during the opening weeks of the war. So every effort was made to attract recruits, including grand military demonstrations, public meetings and regular appeals at workplaces, music halls and cinemas. One of the most successful tactics for drawing in the crowds proved to be open-air concerts held around the city and performed by military bands. The target was achieved by early January 1915 when the 16th (Service) Battalion (Cardiff City) The Welsh Regiment was complete, but it had taken eight weeks of hard effort.

Despite what is sometimes asserted, the title had nothing to do with the Cardiff City Football Club, which had no direct involvement in raising the battalion. Professional soccer was still being played in 1914-15, so the campaign had included appeals to spectators at Cardiff City's Southern League matches at Ninian Park, though these efforts proved to be disappointing. There were no appeals at the Arms Park, however, because rugby had been officially suspended from the outset of war. After Cardiff RFC cancelled all fixtures in August 1914, they even attempted, unsuccessfully as it turned out, to raise a "Sportsmen's" battalion. Nevertheless, if any sports club had close ties with the City Battalion, it was Cardiff RFC. They donated a full set of kit and boots to the 16th Welsh, while battalion members included Cardiff and Wales players Bert Winfield, Clem Lewis, and Dick Thomas. Other "Blue and Blacks" who served in the battalion were Wenvoe-born Lieutenant Robert Duncan, who was capped by England after the war; and Private Alfred Titt, who was killed at Mametz Wood. Johnny would also have known two fellow officers who had played for Glamorgan Wanderers, William Jenkin Richards and Frank Bracher, both of whom died in the war. And second-in-command of the City Battalion was Cardiff's Welsh trialist, Major Fred Smith. So with the battalion still looking for suitable officers, Johnny was an ideal acquisition. In mid-December, he was discharged from The Royal Fusiliers and appointed to a commission in the Cardiff City Battalion. Soon after joining, he and Bert Winfield and Clem Lewis all played for the 16th Welsh against the 11th South Wales Borderers.

Johnny trained with the City Battalion throughout 1915 at Colwyn Bay,

CARDIFF CITY BATTALION: INSPECTION BY THE LORD MAYOR.

A very grainy but rare visual record of the 16th Welsh parading at the Arms Park in 1915. The goal posts at the Westgate Street end and the Cardiff and County Club on the right can just be made out.

Winchester and Salisbury Plain. He proved to be an efficient officer and, within two months, was promoted twice to the rank of captain. Just before going overseas, the 16th Welsh returned to their home city for a final visit to their loved ones. There was only one possible venue for the battalion to parade before a large admiring audience and that, of course, was the Arms Park, where "Johnny Bach" had enthralled his many fans so often. There was also time for the officers to pose briefly for a photograph on the steps of the Law Courts and then they were on their way. The battalion embarked for France on 4 December 1915 as part of the 115th Brigade, 38th (Welsh) Division.

Johnny spent his first few months of war north of Loos, where, in an interesting role reversal, Lieutenant Colonel Fred Smith, his vice-captain at Cardiff in 1909-10, was now his commanding officer. We know, however, that when out of the line, the battalion still had time for rugby because in the February, Johnny had a ball sent out for inter-platoon competition and it was not just *any* ball but his treasured souvenir from the 1911 French match.

The thirty-four year-old Johnny moved south towards the Somme with his battalion in June 1916. There, on 7 July, alongside Dick Thomas, he took part in the Cardiff City Battalion's ill-fated assault on Mametz Wood. Caught by withering fire from the two copses on their right and from the wood itself, the men of the 16th Welsh stood little chance and were cut down before they could reach their objective. Bravely leading his company into the murderous storm, Captain John Lewis Williams became one of the battalion's 300 casualties when he was severely wounded by shrapnel in his

Cardiff City Battalion officers pose on the steps of Cardiff Law Courts, just before going overseas. Johnny is front right. Lieutenant Colonel Gaskell is in the centre; Major Fred Smith on his right.

Johnny Williams, captain of Wales in 1911, with the ball which returned to France in 1916.

left leg. At what point in the attack this happened is not certain. If near the parapet, he might have been scrambled back to the safety of the trench. If, however, he was hit nearer the enemy, he may have had to endure an agonising and long wait in a shell-hole before he could be safely rescued, and this would have greatly increased the risk of infection. When he was eventually brought in, he was in a very bad state and was taken down to No 5 Casualty Clearing Station, located about twelve miles to the south-west at Corbie. Here his wounds were found to be so severe that his left leg had to be amputated. Afterwards, he was able to write to his wife of only eighteen months and tell her that he was in good spirits. But, no doubt with infection setting in, his condition rapidly deteriorated and, sadly, he succumbed to his wounds, five days after the attack, on 12 July 1916. He is buried in Corbie Communal Extension Cemetery along with 900 others, most of whom also died there of wounds received during the Battle of the Somme. "Johnny Bach", the prolific try-scorer, the "universal favourite" of the Arms Park crowd, and one of the undoubted stars of Welsh rugby, had given his life for his country.

John Lewis Williams's headstone in Corbie Communal Cemetery Extension, where many of the burials were placed close together.   [Gwyn Prescott]

Philip Dudley Waller

Born: Bath 28 January 1889.
Died of wounds: Beaumetz-lès-Cambrai 14 December 1917.

Teams: Carmarthen Intermediate School; Newport; Wanderers (Johannesburg); Monmouthshire; Somerset; Great Britain 1910.

Wales: 6 caps, 1908-1910.

The tradition of observing two minutes silence on Armistice Day and Remembrance Sunday was initiated on the suggestion of the South African statesman Sir Percy Fitzpatrick, who had suffered his own grievous loss in the Great War. On 14 December 1917, his son Major Percy Nugent Fitzpatrick, the commanding officer of the 71st (South African) Siege Battery Royal Garrison Artillery, was travelling with a fellow officer in the battery car to a nearby railhead when it was struck by a stray shell near Beaumetz-lès-Cambrai. Major Fitzpatrick was killed instantaneously. His companion, twenty-eight year-old Lieutenant Philip Dudley Waller died shortly afterwards. The battery history recorded: "The loss of these two officers was heavily felt in the battery, both being exceedingly popular."

As an English-born officer in the South African military, Phil Waller may seem an unlikely subject for a book about Welsh rugby. But place of birth has never excessively bothered selectors. Phil was born in 1889 at Odd Down, Bath. His father was employed by the Inland Revenue and his work took the family around the country. By the turn of the century, however, the Wallers had moved to Carmarthenshire, so Phil began playing at Carmarthen Intermediate (Queen Elizabeth Grammar) School. In 1906, when he was seventeen, he left home to become an apprentice engineer with the Alexandra Docks and Railway Company in Newport. This was to be a life-changing event as there he began working under Tom Pearson, a former Welsh international winger.

It was Pearson who recruited Phil for Newport. There he gained his first experience of the adult game with the Thirds and he was eventually promoted to the First XV at the end of 1906-7, participating in a 25-3 victory over London Welsh when he had only just turned eighteen. Over the next three seasons, he became a regular choice in the Newport pack, taking part in seventy-nine First XV matches altogether, including the 5-3 defeat by the Australians in 1908-9. By then, despite his youth, he had become one of the club's leading forwards and during that season he was rewarded for his consistent performances with his Welsh cap. Though never a strong scrummager, he more than made up for this with his line-out play and particularly his mobility in the loose – "a very dashing forward" with "a great capacity for covering work" was how Townsend Collins summed him up.

Newport Athletic Club War Memorial gates, Rodney Parade. [Siân Prescott]

Phil took part in all five internationals in 1908-9. It was a season of which he, and Welsh rugby, could justifiably be proud. The team won all their matches, not only achieving the Grand Slam but also recording a victory over southern hemisphere opposition. They were also the first team to win a consecutive Triple Crown/Grand Slam. And yet, they were not always given their full due. Some journalists suggested they were not a great side and were rather fortunate to enjoy such success. It may well be that the high standard of previous campaigns was not always maintained but, whatever the truth, in terms of results, it cannot be disputed that Phil Waller was a member – as were Johnny Williams and Dick Thomas – of one of the most successful Welsh teams ever. In the history of the Welsh game, only Mervyn Davies's great side of 1975-6 can match their record of Grand Slam and southern hemisphere scalp. Phil is therefore one of only a handful of Welsh players who have ever achieved this.

Consistent displays for Newport and an outstanding performance against the Wallabies for Somerset, when he shone in the line-outs, mauls and loose, convinced the selectors they should include him in the Welsh XV to meet

Australia on 12 December 1908. Pre-match, there was no great optimism about Wales's prospects. The general feeling was that standards had fallen. Before the team was announced, "Old Stager" argued that the stronger scrummaging of Cardiff's Fred Smith should be preferred over the "dash and speed" of Waller. He did concede, however, that Phil was certain to be capped eventually – he was, after all, still only nineteen. He was "fast, has an eye for an opening and is a rattling good man in a (forward) rush". Not for the first or last time though, the selectors thought differently from the press and the youngster found himself named in a somewhat experimental team which relied more on speed than on scrummaging power. Smith, incidentally, never did play for Wales, though, as we have seen, he appears elsewhere in this story as the commanding officer of the Cardiff City Battalion at Mametz Wood. "Old Stager" was indignant, however, that the selectors had overlooked Dick Thomas.

On the Thursday before the international, both teams had a run-out at the Arms Park where, in the days before cryotherapy chambers and training camps in Poland, the pre-match preparation was a relaxed affair, judging from "Old Stager's" account:

> They indulged in muscle stretching practice, forwards opposing backs in dribbling and passing ... the forwards, too, formed a few scrimmages, but unlike the Wallabies, who have had their reserves to play against while trying packing arrangements and practising quick hooking and heeling, the Welshmen had little chance because they were opposed only by nondescript youths who had clambered over the walls and volunteered for the task.

It seems that in all Wales's games this season, the forwards struggled in the set scrummage (though, it is hoped, not against Cardiff's nondescript adolescents) but they more than compensated for this with their vigorous loose play, in which Phil in particular was conspicuous. Despite the pessimism of some pundits, however, the match-day excitement in Cardiff was as great as ever and one supporter was so keen to get to the game that he travelled alone from Swindon in a specially chartered train!

As it turned out, it was a very close game which could have gone either way and it was not without controversy. Wales opened the scoring with a try by George Travers, following some quality play from Dicky Owen and Billy Trew. There was no dispute about this at the time but afterwards it was claimed that Travers had failed to ground the ball. He vehemently denied this, insisting that, after he had touched down, the ball was kicked out of his hands and he added that the referee was perfectly sighted. Tom Richards then equalised for Australia. Phil Carmichael's conversion failed, though he later claimed in a letter to the Welsh press that the ball had gone over. In the second half, Wales went ahead again after Tom Evans charged down a kick and he and Waller followed up with a dribble down field, before winger Phil Hopkins grabbed the ball and scored. Bert Winfield again missed the conversion but compensated for this later with what turned out to be the deciding penalty goal. The Australians now put Wales under great pressure and came back with a try but, in an intensely exciting final period, Wales defended heroically and hung on to their 9-6 lead. The game was largely played in good spirit, though there was one disgraceful incident when Billy Trew had to go off for treatment after Albert

Phil aged nineteen on his Welsh debut.

Burge had kicked him in the head. Ugly scenes of retaliation were just averted and, though Burge should have been dismissed, the referee decided that the kick was accidental. One journalist with the Wallabies wrote that, although the Welsh pack were well beaten in the scrums, they "showed a decided advantage in the fast open rushes and ruck work". We can be sure of Phil's contribution here for, in a post-match interview, the Australian manager singled him out for special praise.

England at Cardiff were next up. They had not beaten Wales for eleven seasons and they failed to improve on this dismal record, though they made it a closer game than expected. With the forwards in sparkling form in the loose, if not in the set scrums, Wales extended their run of victories with an 8-0 scoreline. In Edinburgh, the match was much tighter and Wales just scraped home 5-3. Phil was again prominent, making a particularly valuable contribution to the defence. "All the forwards played with dogged determination but Waller most often caught the eye of the crowd" according to "Old Stager". Even against France, the Welsh pack initially struggled to win the ball in the scrums, but eventually they did get on top and Wales secured one of their most clear-cut of victories, running riot with eleven tries ("as easy as shelling peas"). To this day, 47-5 is their greatest margin of victory in the fixture.

The climax of the season took place at St. Helens, where victory was assured during an astonishing six minute spell in the second half when the Irish line was crossed three times. Phil was involved in two of these scores. He made the second try when he chased and grabbed a loose ball and fed

A poor image from Wales v Australia but which nevertheless testifies to Phil's great line-out work.

Jim Watts who went over. Then he broke away from a line-out and, on half-way, gave to Billy Trew, who ran through the entire Irish team to touch down. Wales eventually won by 18 points to 5. *The Times* was impressed with the Welsh pack's work in the loose and line-outs, two aspects of play where the Irish usually excelled. "The Welsh rushes were marked by a greater combination and control of the ball" though, where Wales were traditionally dominant, "in the tight ... the Irish forwards were superior." Nevertheless, despite the pre-season concerns about the scrummage, Wales had managed to secure a consecutive Triple Crown and Grand Slam; while Phil had totally justified the selectors' faith in him.

He returned to Swansea again for the first international the following season held on New Year's Day 1910. He had been putting in some good displays for Newport so his selection against France was no surprise though it was reported that he had been preferred chiefly because of his work in open play, implying there were questions about his scrummaging. The French had suffered from a rough journey and did not put up much of a fight but even so the Welsh eight did not scrummage at all well. Wales were criticised for not taking the game seriously but they still managed eleven tries, while Jack Bancroft celebrated a record nineteen points in a shattering 49-14 victory. This was Wales's eleventh consecutive win, a

Wales v England 1909. Back: J Blackmore, J Brown, G Travers, AJ Webb, G Hayward, TH Evans; Middle: PD Waller, JP Jones, J Bancroft, W Trew, P Hopkins, JL Williams, WI Morgan; Front Row: R Owen, R Jones. [WRU]

record which has never since been surpassed. Shockingly, of the French XV that day, no fewer than six were to become victims of the war.[1] While Britain's losses in the conflict were appalling – around three-quarters of a million men – the French suffered almost twice as many deaths. With twenty-one internationals killed, the war was particularly costly for French rugby, particularly when it is remembered that France only began playing internationals in 1906 and had capped only 114 players by 1914.

The 1910 French match turned out to be Phil's last game for Wales. The selectors now determined to place more emphasis on the scrum, so he lost his place to the Cardiff docker, Joe Pugsley, who was reckoned to be his equal in the loose but a stronger scrummager. So Phil ended his Welsh international career with an admirable record of six wins out of six. He was still only twenty, so more caps would surely have followed had circumstances not led to his leaving Wales.

Though he had fallen out of favour with the Welsh selectors, he was nevertheless one of seven Newport players chosen for the British tour of South Africa in the summer of 1910. There had been seven previous British tours to the southern hemisphere, but this was the first team officially selected by, and representative of, the four Home Unions. Even so, of the

---

1   They were: Joseph Anduran, René Boudreaux, Marcel Burgun, Pierre Guillemin, Gaston Lane and Alfred Mayssonnié.

Phil Waller in 1910.

original squad of twenty-six, Phil was one of only fourteen who had previously been capped.

One of the uncapped tourists was a Welsh outside-half not well known in Wales. Noel Humphreys, who did not take part in the Tests, had been born in Llangan, near Cowbridge, where his father was the vicar but who later moved to Durham. As a result, Noel played all his rugby in England. Demonstrating that the RFU were no more fixated about country of birth than were the WRU, he played for the North in an English trial in 1912. Awarded the Military Cross in April 1917, he died of wounds a year later while serving as a captain in the Tank Corps.

It was a bruising tour and several players had to be drafted in to replace the injured. The most unusual of these was the Australian, Tom Richards, who during the 1908-9 Wallabies tour had been an adversary of Phil three times. A fast and versatile forward, he was now living in South Africa. He had previously spent some time in England playing for Bristol and, relying on this very flimsy qualification, he was invited to join the British team and subsequently played in two Test matches with Phil. "Rusty" Richards was awarded the Military Cross for his gallantry serving with the Australians in May 1917. The Test series trophy, which was won so dramatically by the British Lions in Australia in 2013, was inaugurated in 2001 and is justifiably named in honour of this very remarkable sportsman and war hero.

Eric Milroy was another replacement. Amongst Scotland's finest pre-war scrum-halves, he was one of eleven players from the 1914 Calcutta Cup match who did not survive the war.[2] A lieutenant in The Black Watch, he was killed on the Somme at Delville Wood on 18 July 1916. Not far away and just three days earlier, Toby Moll of the 1910 Springboks died when serving as a second lieutenant in The Leicestershire Regiment. He had been wounded the previous day during the same battle which took the life of Welsh international Dai Watts.

Though still only a youngster, Phil's playing record in South Africa was quite exceptional as he took part in all but one of the twenty-four tour fixtures. This tells us a great deal about his resilience and stamina because

---

2   They were: Arthur Dingle, Alfred Maynard, Francis Oakley, Ronald Poulton and James Watson (England); and James Huggan, Eric Milroy, Frederic Turner, William Wallace, John Will and Eric Young (Scotland).

the tour took a severe toll of the other players who were plagued by injuries. After missing the third game, he completed a gruelling sequence of twenty-one consecutive matches, in one period playing four games in eight days. So Phil was in the British team for all three Tests. In the first, they were without "Cherry" Pillman, the English loose forward and star of the tour. In a close and thrilling match, the Springboks just edged out Great Britain by 14 points to 10, Phil's first experience of defeat in international rugby. The South Africans were confident about the second Test but Britain squared the series with an 8 points to 3 victory. Astonishingly, Pillman played out of position at fly-half, but still dominated the match, in which Phil also stood out. Unfortunately, injury affected the third Test. British hopes of taking the series were quickly knocked back when the Newport full-back, Stanley Williams, was carried off in the tenth minute. One of the successes of the tour, his early loss was a devastating blow. Down to fourteen men for most of the game, Great Britain were well beaten by 21 points to 5.

With the tour concluded, Phil was one of several players who did not immediately return home. This was not at all unusual on early tours. Some, like Gwyn Nicholls in Australia in 1899, took the once in a lifetime opportunity to see more of the host country. Others, like Blair Swannell in 1904, stayed on to start a new life. Something of a bruiser from Northampton, Swannell represented Britain against Australia on both the 1899 and 1904 tours, and then went on to play *for* Australia against New Zealand in 1905. A major in the Australian infantry during the war, he was killed leading his men at Gallipoli in 1915. In Phil's case, he decided to settle in Johannesburg after being offered a job as an engineer with the local municipality, where he worked for the next five years. Obviously a desirable recruit, he was snapped up by the local Wanderers club and he later captained them. Not being a sufficiently strong scrummager for the South African game, however, he did not emulate Swannell and go on to represent his new country.

With the war clearly not coming to a quick resolution, Phil decided to enlist as a gunner in the South African Heavy Artillery in August 1915. Arriving in Britain with his battery, he underwent training at Bexhill-on-Sea, East Sussex. The following March, Phil's unit, the 71st (South African) Siege Battery, was mobilised as part of the 44th (South African) Brigade, Royal Garrison Artillery. It was the artillery, rather than the machine-gun, which caused

Newport Athletic Club War Memorial. [Siân Prescott]

most casualties on the Western Front and the specialist role of the RGA was an important one. The 71st Siege Battery, for instance, was equipped with heavy howitzers which launched large high-explosive shells on a high trajectory which then fell causing great destruction to enemy targets such as fortifications, ammunition dumps and railheads.

However, while training continued in England, there was still time for rugby and, just before embarking for the Western Front in late April 1916, Phil played in two important matches. On 4 March, he took part in the South African Heavy Artillery's encounter with a previously undefeated New Zealand Military XV at Queen's Club. With three internationals in the pack (though remarkably none of them Springboks), the South Africans gained a credible 7-0 victory. Playing with Phil was the England international Harold Harrison, who was then commanding the 71st Siege Battery. Also in the team was Reggie Hands, a South African by birth but capped by England in 1910 when at Oxford. A member of a highly talented sporting family, he also played Test cricket but this time for his native country. He died of wounds in 1918. As well as three internationals, this powerful pack also included Frank Mellish who played for both England and South Africa after the war.

A return match took place at Richmond a month later but this time the New Zealanders gained their revenge by 5 points to 3. Perhaps the prospect of going on active service was preying on the minds of the South Africans, because they left for France less than two weeks later. Though this was Phil's last important game, no doubt there were other opportunities for recreational rugby when out of the line.

During his twenty months on the Western Front, Phil was in the thick of action, including major offences at the Somme, Arras, Ypres and Cambrai. His battery initially served around Ypres but, in June 1916, they went south to take part in the bombardment for the opening of the Battle of the Somme. On 5 July 1916, they began supporting the attacks on Ovilliers, Contalmaison and Mametz Wood, so Phil was nearby when his two former Grand Slam colleagues in the Cardiff City Battalion became casualties. The 71st Battery were involved throughout the Battle of the Somme until it finally drew to a close in November 1916.

In early 1917, Phil was engaged in the advance to the Hindenburg Line and the Battle of Arras. After a year's distinguished service, he was then commissioned in the field in May and later promoted to lieutenant. The following September, he went north again to take part in the Third Battle of Ypres. As on the Somme, his battery were in action almost continuously and they suffered heavy casualties supporting the bloody battles of Menin Road, Polygon Wood, Broodseinde and Passchendaele. Despite horrendous losses, these struggles in the frightful conditions at the Salient did not produce the hoped-for breakthrough.

So when Third Ypres eventually petered out in November, the battery was ordered south in great secrecy to Gouzeaucourt in preparation for the Battle of Cambrai. This was a combined-arms attack, involving the mass use of tanks, new infantry tactics, artillery, cavalry and aircraft. The open and undamaged rolling landscape around the strategic railhead of Cambrai provided ideal ground conditions. It was in the aftermath of this battle that Phil Waller lost his life, although he is often said to have died at Arras.

Early on the morning of 20 November 1917, 476 British tanks began rolling towards the German lines. A few minutes later, over 1,000 guns roared into action, though to confuse the enemy, the barrage lasted for only ten

Red Cross Corner Cemetery, near Bapaume. The headstones of Major Fitzpatrick and Lieutenant Waller are in the foreground.   [Gary Williams]

minutes. At first the Germans were taken wholly by surprise and the attack was a staggering success. As a result, Phil's battery later advanced north to Doignies from where they were able to attack Bourlon Wood. On a six mile front, the British penetrated up to five miles into the German lines. In Britain church bells were rung. But the celebrations were premature. The advance could not be reinforced, progress slowed and ultimately there was no breakthrough. Then, on 30 November, the Germans launched a ferocious counter-attack in which they not only won back much of the lost ground but also inflicted heavy casualties on the British. The 71st Battery's guns at Doignies now came under intense shell-fire, so for greater safety, on 7th December, the men's billets were moved a couple of miles west to Beaumetz-lès-Cambrai.

Phil had been lucky to survive this onslaught unharmed, as he had the earlier battles of 1916 and 1917, but no-one was ever completely safe on the Western Front. A little over a week after the Battle of Cambrai ended, Phil was making his way home on leave when he made that fatal journey from Beaumetz with Major Fitzpatrick. A short distance from where they were tragically caught by stray shellfire, they lie alongside each other in the small and beautiful Red Cross Corner Cemetery at Beugny on the Cambrai to Bapaume road.

Philip Waller's headstone. [inmemories.com]

Brinley Richard Lewis

Born: Pontardawe 4 January 1891.
Killed in action: Boesinghe 2 April 1917.

Teams: Swansea Grammar School; Welsh Schoolboys; Pontardawe; Swansea; Trinity Hall, Cambridge; Cambridge University; London Welsh; Glamorgan; Barbarians.

Wales: 2 caps, 1912-1913.

Although "Bryn" Lewis was by no means unknown to the Welsh public, he played much of his best rugby in England, mainly for Cambridge University and occasionally for London Welsh. As a consequence – at least according to EHD Sewell – he was more highly regarded across the border than in Wales:

> It was a very serious feature of his football career, and quite unaccountable to Englishmen and especially Cambridge men, that his powers were not appreciated by the Welsh authorities as they ought to have been. Any number of wings played for Wales during the period 1910-13 who were never in Lewis's class in any branch of wing three-quarter play. He had splendid hands, true football pace, pluck, neat kicking ability ... and he knew the game. He was the best wing of his day in Wales who could boast only a couple of International Caps.

From an early age, Bryn showed great promise. At fourteen, he was already being described as the best three-quarter in schoolboy rugby. He was capped by the Welsh Schoolboys in 1905 and, after they defeated England by 6 points to 0 at Leicester, one match report declared that "Lewis, the big Swansea boy, played brilliantly on the right wing". Ironically, in later life, it was his lack of size which was often commented on.

Pontardawe War Memorial.   [Siân Prescott]

Born in 1891 in Pontardawe, where his family owned the Glantawe tinplate works, Bryn captained the First XV at Swansea Grammar School and was remembered there as a talented sportsman. He was a clever lad too – bright enough to secure a place at Trinity Hall, Cambridge in 1909 to read law. After missing a few early fixtures in his first term, he eventually broke into the Cambridge team and, even though he was only a raw eighteen year-old, he won his place on the left wing against Oxford. However, his first experience of Varsity Match rugby was a distinctly unhappy one. With Ronnie Poulton in commanding form, and despite being down to thirteen men for a time, the Dark Blues overwhelmed Cambridge by 35-3, scoring nine tries in the process, five of them by the incomparable Poulton. Playing in front of a 16,000 crowd at Queen's Club, Bryn defended well but had few opportunities to show what he could do with the ball in hand. The Cambridge backs had not been helped when they were forced to make a late change at centre which disrupted their cohesion.

Pontardawe RFC had a strong fixture list at this time and, during his vacations, Bryn often played for them against teams of the calibre of Aberavon, Pontypool and Llanelli. By the end of 1909-10, he had joined Swansea but he continued to help out his local club when possible. Back in Cambridge, the English press were now taking note. When he scored all three of Cambridge's tries in the draw with Blackheath, for instance, he "was excellent in both defence and attack". There was no doubt that he would retain his place for the 1910 Varsity Match. Oxford were again hot favourites but this time the game turned out to be a desperately close and exciting affair of alternating fortunes. Newport's Billy Geen scored three tries to put Oxford into a 13-0 lead but there was to be no repeat of the previous season's collapse by Cambridge. They began to throw the ball about and they hit back with three tries, the second

Pontardawe War Memorial.   [Siân Prescott]

of which Bryn scored under the posts. Against all predictions, at half-time the Light Blues led 15-13 and they maintained the pressure on Oxford in the second half. Things began to look even brighter when Bryn speedily outflanked the Dark Blues' defence and raced away for his second try. The touchline conversion attempt failed, but Cambridge had now extended their lead to five points and were beginning to look like victors. But then, in the turning point of the match, Bryn was injured and was forced to leave the field for the remainder of the game. His absence allowed the Oxford backs to regain supremacy as Poulton took full advantage of the disorganised Cambridge defence. Twice he struck, both times between the posts. His first try was converted to draw Oxford level. So too was his second which gave them a 23-18 victory in the dying minutes.

Painting of Bryn Lewis in his Cambridge University kit. [Swansea RFC]

A chastened Cambridge now had to lift themselves up for a tough tour of south Wales and Ireland. Although the Welsh leg involved defeats at Swansea and Newport, it gave Bryn the chance to impress the Welsh selectors and he took it. *The Times* thought he might well be selected against England and this seemed more than a possibility when his name appeared in the team lists for the Welsh trial. As it happened, Bryn was one of five current or future internationals who took part in this game and who were destined to die in the war.[1] In the end, Bryn wasn't capped in 1910-11 but he had only just

---

1   The others were Billy Geen, Charlie Pritchard, Dick Thomas and Johnny Williams. Hopkin Maddock who died in 1921 also played.

turned twenty and there was still plenty of time. When not required by Swansea that season, he played again for Pontardawe and was described as "sensational" when they defeated Mountain Ash 3-0 and he also participated in their historic 9-0 win over Llanelli.

His opportunity at international level at last came the following season. Some inspired displays for Cambridge, when he regularly demonstrated his blistering pace, meant that he was now a serious contender for the Welsh wing. In a 24-3 demolition of London Scottish, it was his speed which "represented the difference between the two teams". However, the 1911 Varsity Match turned out to be yet another disappointment, when Bryn found himself on the losing side for the third time. We can never know how the match would have turned out had outside-half Wyndham Thomas been fit. As it was, Cambridge went down to a humiliating 19-0 five-try defeat. Missing Thomas, they played too defensively but at least Bryn could hold his head up high. According to *The Times*, "B.R. Lewis, who was ready to try reverse passes when he had drawn his opponents, alone grasped what was wanted in attack. He was badly served by his centre." "Old Stager" agreed: "Lewis had some good runs, cross kicked cleverly and always showed judgement but was handicapped by the poor play of his fellow backs." The WRU selectors were at the match to assess Bryn and Oxford's Billy Geen. Under a headline "Welshmen in Brilliant Form", "Old Stager" wrote that both had a good chance of being capped against England. As it was, neither did play in the match.

The 1911-12 season marked the end of Welsh rugby's "Golden Era", which had begun way back in 1899-1900. The year started with defeat at Twickenham. This was followed by a much more promising 21-6 win over Scotland at Swansea, where Bryn was a reserve. Then, at last, after several near misses, the selectors decided to call him up to play on the left wing in Belfast. With both half-backs Dicky Owen and Billy Trew dropping out and seven players winning their first caps, it was a great risk taking such an inexperienced side to Ireland and it didn't come off. For the first time in thirteen years, Wales lost two Championship games in a season. The responsibility for the 12-5 defeat was placed squarely on the backs who squandered many scoring opportunities and a surprisingly overawed Bryn Lewis took much of the blame. Hamish Stuart of the *South Wales Daily News* pulled no punches:

> Bryn Lewis was the weakest member of the Welsh team. The failure of Wales was due to two men: Birt (right centre) and Lewis (left wing). Lewis failed to produce his Cambridge form and was probably over-anxious. He overran his centre repeatedly and either missed the ball

or the pass was forward. He lost at least three certain tries by this fault.

"Impossibly feeble" was the *South Wales Daily News*'s final withering assessment. Such remarkably critical comments demonstrate that Welsh rugby players of the period didn't have to be just *physically* tough to survive at the top of the game. It surprised no-one when he was dropped for the French match.

Fortunately for Bryn, he was more than able to make amends for this poor performance the following season, at the beginning of which he returned to Cambridge for a fourth year to complete his law studies. Before going back, he had some good games for Swansea, particularly the crucial 3-0 win over their close rivals Cardiff. He was then picked for the Glamorgan team which met the Springboks at the Arms Park. Suffering from a heavy cold, he wanted to cry off but was prevailed upon to play. Glamorgan went down to a rather humiliating 35-3 defeat to the tourists. Despite being unwell, Bryn scored his team's only points, saved a certain try and

Wales v Ireland 1912. Back: T Williams, WJ Jenkins, L Crump, G Stephens, J Merry, H Hiams; Middle: F Hawkins, H Uzzell, W Davies, J Bancroft, T Vile, R Plummer, F Birt; Front: BR Lewis, W Martin.   [WRU]

touch kicked well, but otherwise he did not feature strongly in what was, after all, a weak all round team display. A few days later, and now fully recovered, he was back to his usual impressive form for the Light Blues. Against London Scottish, he "simply left the opposition standing ... Lewis stood out in a class by himself". He experienced another heavy defeat at the hands of the South Africans, as Cambridge went down 24-0. He was then selected for his fourth Blue but a strained muscle forced him to pull out and so he missed his final chance of a victory against Oxford.

After Christmas he played the rest of the season for Swansea, at last now able to regularly demonstrate his talents to the Welsh public. This was a good season to be playing for the All Whites as they lost only twice in thirty-seven matches and defeated (though without Bryn) the touring Springboks 3-0. There is no doubt that Bryn was coming back into form. He had initially been out of favour with the selectors following his flawed exhibition for Wales in Ireland the previous year. But, for the Irish fixture at Swansea in March, he was reinstated to the left wing – an entirely justifiable decision, according to "Old Stager", given his recent "vastly improved play" for Swansea.

Playing with far greater self-assurance than in his previous international outing, Bryn had a magnificent game at St. Helens. It was a tense match, which the unfancied Irish came close to winning. With the best three-quarter display of that year's Championship, Wales just managed to hang on to a narrow and exciting win by 16 points to 13. Bryn had a big hand in that victory, contributing two of the three Welsh tries, one of which started at half way. He also came close to scoring on several other occasions. He completely made up for his earlier failure by running with great confidence and speed and defending courageously, and he was acknowledged as the best three-quarter on the field. Further honours came over Easter when he made his debut for the Barbarians, though he was unable to stave off an 8-3 defeat by a very much in-form Penarth. However, a few days later he scored two tries for the tourists in their 13-6 win at Cheltenham. Bryn's season then came to a memorable climax as Swansea clinched the 1912-13 Welsh Club Championship.

Following the Ireland match at Swansea, "Old Stager" forecast a bright international future for Bryn "now that he has taken an earnest view of the game instead of the lackadaisical interest he displayed in Belfast and for Glamorgan." But Bryn did not add to his two caps in 1913-14. In the early part of the year, he was missing from the Swansea team on a number of occasions and "Old Stager" renewed his old complaint: "I would like to see him return to Swansea's ranks, for he can do much service for Wales, especially if he can be induced to take his footer a little more seriously, as there is no three-quarter in Wales today with his speed and knowledge of the game". He then withdrew from the trial for the England game and so was not considered by the selectors. "Old Stager" chided, "there will be disappointment doubtless at the absence of Bryn Lewis, (but he) has himself to thank for his omission, for he frequently fails to show sufficient exertion to give full play to his real ability".

Whatever the reason for his absence – which may well have been justified – and for his apparent lack of interest, Bryn then seems to have made every effort to prove his critics wrong. After Christmas he played with greater determination for Swansea, ending the season as the club's top try scorer. Following Swansea's 13-0 victory over Leicester when he crossed for a try, "Old Stager" now recanted and wrote that Bryn appeared to have taken heed of his earlier comments about his indifference on the field. After he scored in the 11-3 defeat of Llanelli, "Old Stager" reported that he was "again conspicuous", adding that if he had only shown this form earlier in the season, he would certainly have been in the Welsh team. In April 1914, Bryn played for the third and last time for the Barbarians, when they again lost by 8 points to 3 at Penarth. Exactly a year later, however, he would find himself playing against the Barbarians in totally different circumstances.

In August 1914, Bryn was settling into his career as an articled clerk to a Swansea solicitor. With his self-confidence restored, a new season

Swansea Cricket and Football Club War Memorial, St. Helens.   [David Dow]

with the All Whites beckoned and, with that, also came the real prospect of representing Wales again. However, the declaration of war immediately put an end to all such speculation and, in October 1914, the twenty-three year-old enlisted as a trooper in the 2/1st Glamorgan Yeomanry, a Territorial Force cavalry unit based at Bridgend.

It was during this period of his Army service that Bryn played his last major match in Britain. In April 1915, a special fixture was arranged at the Arms Park to boost recruitment and raise money for charities. To increase public interest, it was promoted in the press as an unofficial international with England and even the match programme promised spectators a "Grand Military International Match England v Wales". However, it seems that even in rugby, "the first casualty when war comes is truth": the team which the Welsh XV *actually* played was the Barbarians club. Despite the official ban on playing, the Barbarians continued to operate during the early months of the war, playing charity matches and selecting teams made up of men on military service or engaged on war work. The Welsh match was the fifth such game for the Barbarians but, with so many of the personnel eventually going overseas, they wound up their "war services" matches in November 1915. Sixty-five Barbarians – including Bryn Lewis of course – made the supreme sacrifice. The Barbarians team which faced the Welsh XV was certainly not completely English. It included: two existing Irish internationals and a future one; Welsh-born "Birdie" Partridge who was capped by South Africa in 1903; and R. Lennox Davies of London Welsh. Four of the team had played for England and the side was captained by Edgar Mobbs.

On paper, Wales selected a strong and representative team. Only two had not been capped, while five of the backs and five of the "Terrible Eight" – including Dai Watts – had played in the extreme roughhouse in Ireland a year earlier. Bryn Lewis came into the side on the wing and proved to be one of the few Welsh successes on the day. Unhappily for Wales, the issue was never in doubt from the first few moments and they were trounced by 26 points to 10. The *Western Mail* lamented that it had been a long time since a Welsh XV had been so thoroughly beaten in Cardiff. What was clearly hard to take though was that the Barbarians had beaten the Welsh at their own game with a "delightful exhibition of fast, open football". Amongst the better Welsh players, though, were the try-scorers, Ivor Davies and Bryn Lewis. Both wings "made full use of the few opportunities given them by using their speed along the touch line." Nevertheless, the Welsh performance was a major let-down after expectations had been so raised in 1913-14. The Barbarians' history admits that the visitors were remarkably fit, as fourteen of them had been in training in the Army and most had been playing in military matches. Even so, at least ten of the Welshmen were also in the services, though how much "game time" they had had is not known. The lack of cohesion and understanding which characterised the Welsh play can only be explained by rustiness and lack of match fitness. Nevertheless, the fixture was a clear success in its main objectives: over 160 men enlisted and £245 was donated to military charities.

Fed up with kicking his heels on "Home Defence" and anxious to go on active service, shortly after the Barbarians match, Bryn took matters into his own hands and applied for a commission in the Welsh Division artillery. This was granted with effect from 1 May 1915. The first unit of the division's artillery had begun forming in Cardiff in late 1914, however, by the time Bryn joined, the gunners had been based in north Wales for several months. As a "New Army" formation, all the units of the Welsh Division suffered from shortages, not least the artillery. For some time, they

Wales v Barbarians ("England") match programme, 1915. [David Dow]

had no guns and were even forced at one stage to practise limbering up with old bus wheels. Later in the year, they moved to the south of England and, by the end of August, the whole of the 38th (Welsh) Division were located in the Winchester area, where they underwent more advanced training.

However, when the time came for embarking overseas, the divisional artillery had to be held back in Britain because the shortages meant they hadn't yet been able to practise with live ammunition. As a consequence, the four field artillery brigades, numbered 119 to 122, left for France some three weeks after the rest of the 38th (Welsh) Division. And so it was that, on Christmas morning 1915, Lieutenant Brinley Lewis found himself overseeing the tricky business of disembarking C Battery 120 Brigade Royal Field Artillery at Le Havre. He and the rest of the artillery then moved to the Neuve Chapelle area to re-join their comrades of the Welsh Division. They spent the whole of January acclimatising, with detachments of all four batteries being regularly drafted for instruction by other artillery units already in the firing line. Then, on 31 January 1916, the four brigades relieved the 19th Division artillery and took over responsibility for the line together for the first time. Over the next six months, Bryn was engaged in shelling enemy positions around Neuve Chapelle, Festubert and Givenchy. Though the conditions there were generally not good, it was at least a relatively quiet sector for the gunners. In mid-June, though, the Welsh Division was pulled out of the line and ordered south to the Somme. There Bryn fought in the Battle of Mametz Wood, supporting the infantry in their bloody, but eventually successful, assault on that truly formidable enemy stronghold.

In August 1916, the Welsh Division moved from the Somme to Belgium and took over the line in the Ypres Salient opposite Pilckem Ridge. Three months later, despite being only twenty-five, Bryn was posted commanding officer of the six-gun B Battery 122 Brigade RFA. Along with this went promotion from lieutenant to major – clear evidence of his leadership and technical skills, since being promoted directly to major without first becoming a captain was unusual. The Welsh Division served around the Boesinghe area throughout the winter of 1916-17 but, as well as fighting the enemy, the troops also had to battle the elements. The weather was abysmal: at various times they suffered from the wet, the mud, the frost, and the bitterly freezing conditions. There were constant raids and counter-raids to contend with. And, of course, there was always hostile shell-fire.

A game of rugby, though, could always be relied on to dispel all the miseries for a moment, and Bryn might well have played for the Welsh Division XV which lost 18-7 to the New Zealand Division in the March. If so, however, this would have provided him with only a temporary respite. Just two weeks later on 2 April 1917, Major Brinley Lewis was relaxing at breakfast with a fellow officer, Second Lieutenant David Carnegie, when they were suddenly hit by a high velocity shell meant for a battery some 300 yards to the rear. He and Carnegie were killed instantaneously and they are today buried next to each other in Ferme-Olivier Cemetery, Elverdinge,

Ferme-Olivier Cemetery, Elverdinge, near Ypres. [britishcemeteries.webs.com]

near Boesinghe. They lie not far from Artillery Wood Cemetery, which is the last resting place of the Welsh poet Hedd Wyn, who also served in the 38th (Welsh) Division. They also lie near Langemark, where a Welsh national memorial, part-funded by the Welsh Government and dedicated to all those from Wales killed during the Great War will, proudly and poignantly, complement the evocative and magnificent memorial to the 38th (Welsh) Division at Mametz Wood, which was established by the South Wales Branch of the Western Front Association.

Shortly after Bryn's death, he was Mentioned in Despatches, while his brigade commander Lieutenant Colonel William Rudkin sent this personal tribute to his next of kin:

> He was such a splendid fellow, and he cannot be replaced. He has done magnificent work since he had been given command of "B" Battery: he had shown great powers of leadership, and he was beloved by officers and men alike. I had him specially promoted from subaltern to Major, as I knew he would take responsibility. He had great strength of character and was bound to do well always.

Welsh Championship and Barbarians honours, Cambridge Blues, Welsh caps – Bryn Lewis achieved much in the game in his twenty-six years, but there can be little doubt that the Great War robbed this exciting winger – and indeed Wales – of so much more.

Bryn Lewis's headstone.   [britishcemeteries.webs.com]

Horace Wyndham Thomas

Born: Pentyrch 28 July 1890.
Killed in action: Ancre 3 September 1916.

Teams: Bridgend County School; Monmouth School; King's College, Cambridge; Cambridge University; Blackheath; London Welsh; Swansea; Calcutta; Barbarians.

Wales: 2 caps, 1912-1913.

Apart from players who had the misfortune to suffer a serious injury, few in the history of rugby football can have experienced a more sudden and dramatic departure from the international game than Horace Wyndham (otherwise known as "Wyndham" or "H.W.") Thomas. Just two days before he was due to win his first cap against South Africa on 14 December 1912, it was announced that he had secured a five-year appointment with a firm of shipping agents in Calcutta and he would be sailing from Gravesend on 18 January. By coincidence, this was also the very date of the next international match against England at the Arms Park. This caused some consternation in the WRU but eventually a way was found to enable him to play for Wales *and* travel to India on time. It was complicated and it asked a lot of the talented young outside-half but it demonstrates the high regard in which he was held.

Not long after the final whistle in the England match, Wyndham headed for the station to catch his connection to the cross-channel ferry to France. He then travelled overland to Marseilles where he managed to join his ship while she briefly docked en route for India. So one minute he was playing at the peak of his career in the maelstrom of a Wales v England international in front of thousands of wildly enthusiastic supporters. Then, suddenly, it was all over and he was on his way, not only out of the country, but also out of senior rugby forever. When Wyndham did eventually return to Britain three years later, international sport was no longer a priority.

There is little doubt that, as far as Welsh rugby is concerned, Horace Wyndham Thomas was one who got away. EHD Sewell believed he would have been the regular outside-half for Wales had he not gone overseas:

> He was a very fine attacking stand-off half with a very quick change of foot, excellent hands, a good pass, and a keen intuition of the right game to play ... without being numbered among the great tacklers, (he) had defensive ability considerably stouter than is usually seen in Welsh stand-off half backs ... as a player and as a man (he) was extremely popular. As an example to future generations that of this brilliant young Cantab stands out as a beacon. He would, indeed, have gone far.

Tragically, he was prevented from fulfilling his enormous potential and his departure was a great loss to the game.

Wyndham was born in 1890 into a Welsh-speaking family in Pentyrch, near Cardiff. His father was the local schoolmaster who later became curate of the village. A "muscular Christian", Reverend Morgan Thomas believed in the moralising influence of vigorous sports. Keen on taking his pupils to watch cricket and rugby, in the spring of 1883 he helped set up Pentyrch RFC and acted as the club secretary for some years. So Wyndham grew up in a religious household but it was also one in which participation in sport was actively encouraged.

In 1900, his father was appointed curate of Llantrisant and, in the same year, Wyndham enrolled at Bridgend County (Grammar) School where he eventually captained the rugby team. The headmaster described him as "the finest character we ever had here", and so must have been sorry to see him leave to take up a scholarship at Monmouth in January 1906. There he became one of the school's most talented all-rounders, not only starring in the First XV but also representing Monmouth at athletics and captaining them at cricket, hockey and gymnastics.

By no means, however, were his talents confined to the sports field. A highly proficient musician, Wyndham won a choral scholarship to King's College, Cambridge in 1909, although he did not take this up until late in the academic year, entering King's in January 1910. Having missed the first term, initially there was little time for serious sport, because he had to concentrate on his chorister's duties and catch up with his studies. These had to be his priorities. Many students attending Cambridge before the First World War had no pretence to scholarship and, for men more interested in games, taking an "Ordinary" degree was a perfectly acceptable choice.

However, this option wasn't available to Wyndham as it might have been in some other colleges. At King's, everyone had to read for an Honours degree.

In due course, however, Wyndham was able to throw himself wholeheartedly into undergraduate life, as evidenced by his obituary in the King's College Annual Report of 1916 which could not have been more generous in its praise:

Wyndham as a schoolboy.

> Probably no undergraduate ever had a happier or fuller life than he did ... He was an excellent musician and delighted in the services of the Chapel, he was a good cricketer and had a real genius for Rugby football, he acted, and acted well, both for the A.D.C. and the Marlowe Society, he was the friend of all ... Every quality he had he used to the full and he was always the same simple kind modest boy, where another might easily have been spoilt and vain ... Of all the losses which the College has sustained in the war, perhaps none has affected so many of different ages and different classes as the death of H.W. Thomas.

When it is remembered that among the many losses which King's had already suffered by this date was the poet Rupert Brooke, the sentiment expressed in this tribute is as remarkable as it is moving.

His versatility was perhaps his most engaging characteristic. His unique combination of talents enabled him, unusually, to mix equally well with both "hearties" and "aesthetes", not necessarily an easy feat in Cambridge at that time. The world-famous Festival of Nine Lessons and Carols was not introduced until 1918 but the pre-war King's Chapel choir still had a very demanding programme of college services and concerts. Despite these heavy commitments, however, he still found time to act and sing in a variety of theatrical productions staged either by the Amateur Dramatic Club or the more serious Marlowe Society, which Rupert Brooke had helped to found. Since Wyndham possessed the rare countertenor voice, he was sometimes called on to perform female roles. Though Rupert Brooke left King's just before Wyndham went up to university, he stayed in Cambridge and remained involved in Marlowe Society circles, so they may well have been acquaintances. On top of all this, he still found time to play cricket for King's, Cambridge University Second XI and, when at home, the Earl of Plymouth's XI at St. Fagans.

At the beginning of the 1910-11 season, he was at last able to apply himself seriously to rugby. He joined Blackheath and soon made quite an impact there. In their 26-8 victory over Richmond, *The Times* reported that he "was more or less responsible for most of Blackheath's (six) tries" and predicted that he would go far in the game. He continued to assist Blackheath, when not required by the Light Blues, until he left for India. Despite the good reviews, he was initially ignored by the Varsity selectors but eventually his class was recognised and in the following season, 1911-12, he established himself as the Cambridge outside-half. Regularly praised by the press, this was an exciting time for Wyndham. On the strength of his games for Cambridge against Swansea and Newport, he was selected reserve for the Welsh trial even before he had won his Blue. Everything was going swimmingly but then Wyndham suffered a huge disappointment when he was injured in the last few minutes of the final game before the Varsity Match. Though named in the 1911 Cambridge XV to play Oxford, he was forced to withdraw, costing him his Blue. Fortunately, Wyndham recovered quite quickly and was invited to join the Barbarians' Christmas tour, appearing in their fixtures with Newport and Leicester. His debut at Rodney Parade was the first time the Welsh public were able to judge for themselves whether the English press had been exaggerating. He did not disappoint, on one occasion intercepting a pass and cheekily kicking over the Newport full-back's head to score a try.

When Swansea had played at Cambridge in November 1911, he had come to the attention of none other than Dicky Owen, hero of the Welsh victory over New Zealand. Swansea won 12-9 but Wyndham nearly clinched the match for the Light Blues with a drop goal that just missed – an event which would be repeated on a much more important stage a year later. After the game, Owen told reporters that he was impressed by Wyndham's elusiveness and by the way he opened up defences. He thought he was the best all-round outside-half he had met that season and hoped that he would get the chance to partner him soon. He predicted that Wyndham would one day play for Wales and, coming from one of the finest scrum-halves of any era, this high praise was noted by the Welsh selectors. Because of his choral duties, Wyndham had to spend much of his vacation in Cambridge, but over Christmas 1911 he made a short visit home to Bettws near Bridgend where his father was now rector. This meant Owen's wish could now be realised and Wyndham came in as a late replacement for Swansea in their game at Bristol. He made some good breaks but disappointingly the two did not combine well. Playing poorly, the Welsh club went down to an unexpected and, for the All Whites, a somewhat humiliating 3-0 defeat. Before returning to King's, Wyndham had only one more game for Swansea in their nil-all

Monmouth School War Memorial.   [Gwyn Prescott]

draw at Llanelli. The experiment was not repeated. These were his only two appearances for the club, though he is usually inaccurately described as a Swansea player when he was capped a year later. His game at Stradey Park was – after his appearance at Rodney Parade for the Barbarians – the second and last time he played in a senior club match in Wales.

Although Wyndham passed his final history exams in the summer of 1912, he did not leave King's immediately. In order to qualify for a B.A. degree at Cambridge, one of the archaic regulations of the University requires that an undergraduate must have been in residence for nine terms. Since he had only completed eight, he therefore had to return for a final, but exam-free, term in the autumn. For Wyndham, though, this was no burdensome imposition, since it gave him the chance at last to win the rugby Blue he so richly deserved. So he was able to retain the Cambridge outside-half spot for the 1912-13 season and the good reports continued. "Brilliant" now became an almost over-used description, while Wyndham was variously referred to as "constantly bewildering", "the life and soul of the side" and possessing "a wonderful knack of breaking away from a crowd when apparently hopelessly hemmed in". Reading such comments, as well reports of his promising form for the Light Blues against the Springboks, the Welsh selectors sensibly decided to delay their announcement of the half-backs to play against South Africa until they had watched Wyndham's performance in the Varsity Match. This was a highly controversial decision, as the game took place only four days before the international and his selection (and indeed that of Oxford's Billy Geen) would contravene the WRU's own ban on playing during the week before a match. It demonstrates, however, the fine reputation that Wyndham (and Billy) now enjoyed.

In searching for evidence of the devastating affect which the war had on sport, one need look no further than the 1912 Varsity Match. Of the thirty participants, twenty-eight fought in the war and thirteen were destined to die, nine of them internationals.[1] Wyndham was one of seven Light Blues who fell. Reunions at post-war Varsity Matches must have been deeply melancholy affairs.

Bryn Lewis was injured, so although he and Wyndham were close contemporaries at Cambridge, they never played in a Varsity Match together. This time, however, Cambridge ended a long period of Oxford success with a 10-3 win. Wyndham had few chances to make breaks, though he made the best of those which came his way and he kicked well throughout. He certainly did enough to impress all eight Welsh selectors who were unanimous that he should play against South Africa. There were subsequent complaints about this, as some years earlier, the WRU had resolved to give preference to those who played for London Welsh rather than other London clubs. Wyndham may have had the odd game for London Welsh but, like Billy Geen, he threw in his lot with Blackheath and it made little sense to rule them both out of selection just because of this. Wyndham's scrum-half partner for the international was Tommy Vile. The two had never played together before and they only had time for one short practice at Newport on the day before the match: they did things differently then. Among the six new caps in the forwards was Fred Perrett of Neath, so of this Welsh

---

1   Seven from Cambridge died: WHB Baxter; PCB Blair (Scotland); AF Maynard (England); HW Thomas (Wales); WM Wallace (Scotland); JG Will (Scotland); and AH Wilson. Six from Oxford: DM Bain (Scotland); EF Boyd; WM Dickson (Scotland); WP Geen (Wales); SSL Steyn (Scotland); and FW Thomson.

Wales v South Africa 1912. Back: B Hollingdale, F Andrews, Rees Thomas, JL Morgan, FL Perrett, HW Thomas; Middle: WH Wetter, W Spiller, R Plummer, T Vile, PL Jones, G Stephens, WP Geen; Front: RF Williams; F Birt. ` *[WRU]*

XV three made the ultimate sacrifice, as did two of the Springboks, Jacky Morkel and Tommy Thompson.

Wales had not lost at the Arms Park for thirteen years and they were fired up to make amends for their unexpected defeat by the Springboks in 1906. They very nearly succeeded this time. The only score came from a South African penalty after Rees Thomas accidentally went off-side at a maul. Wales squandered a couple of try-scoring opportunities, while Fred Birt, who had kicked all of Newport's points in their splendid 9-3 victory over the Springboks, missed an easy equaliser. *The Times* noted that Wyndham was very closely marked throughout but thought he did enough to justify his selection. Then, with time running out, Wyndham made a desperate attempt to pull the game out of the fire. About fifteen yards in from touch and thirty yards out, he dropped for goal. Success would have put Wales into a 4-3 lead with only five minutes remaining. A great roar went up but the referee signalled no goal. Though many fans – and some neutral journalists – disagreed, it was judged that Wyndham had missed the upright by six inches. Wales lost by a narrow margin. It is hard to disagree with the *Western Mail*'s assessment: "(he is) just the type of player Wales cannot afford to lose ... those inches were sufficient to deprive Wales of victory and of making the brilliant Cantab one of the immortals of Welsh football." Just like Charles Taylor in 1884, Wyndham had been robbed of rugby glory.

Wyndham played in farewell matches for Cambridge, Blackheath and the Barbarians over Christmas, while he re-arranged his travel plans so that he could wear the Welsh jersey once more. He must have relished the opportunity of representing his country against so many familiar English players, especially as England had never previously won in Cardiff. But this time they proved too good for Wales and fully deserved their 12-0 victory. The Welsh half-backs were closely marked by "Cherry" Pillman, while the wet and muddy conditions made passing difficult. Even so, Wyndham still managed to make several good breaks and he kicked well to his wings. *The Times* reported that he was responsible for most of Wales's dangerous movements. He had a good defensive game too.

This disappointing result, though, signalled the end of Wyndham's senior career. He continued to play in India where for two seasons he captained the Calcutta club with some success but obviously the standard there was not particularly demanding for an outside-half of such extraordinary ability. It should come as no surprise to learn that not all his energies were taken up by rugby while overseas. He played cricket for Calcutta; he regularly performed solos in the city's Cathedral; and he also gave up much of his spare time organising and participating in entertainments and concerts in support of local charities. In addition, as soon as war broke out, Wyndham enlisted as a private in the Calcutta Port Defence Volunteers. However, when it became clear that the fighting was going to drag on, in November 1915 he resigned from both his job and the Volunteers and caught the boat back home. He immediately headed for Cambridge, where his application for a commission was supported by the Vice-Provost of King's – who was later knighted for his zeal in helping to recruit young men for the Army – and he underwent a medical examination in the town.

On 4 January 1916, he was posted to the 14th (Reserve) Battalion The Rifle Brigade which was then based at Seaford, Sussex and which supplied drafts for the battalions of the regiment at the front. He was later attached to the 16th (Service) Battalion (St. Pancras) The Rifle Brigade which had gone overseas on 8 March 1916 as part of the 117th Brigade, 39th Division. They spent a few months in the trenches around Givenchy and Festubert where Wyndham joined them on 12 June. Then in August the battalion moved south to the Somme where they underwent training in the back area before moving to the forward zone in readiness for the "Attack Astride the Ancre".

Here, on 3 September 1916, the 16th Rifle Brigade was engaged in the 39th Division's assault up the left bank of the Ancre. Simultaneously, on the right of the river, the 49th (West Riding) Division attacked the hamlet of St. Pierre Divion. The task of Wyndham's Division was to capture three lines of trenches on high ground above the Ancre, in order to prevent the West Riding Division from being exposed to flanking fire from their left as they advanced up the Ancre valley. With great gallantry, some of the 39th Division's troops managed to secure the enemy's front trench but the 16th Rifle Brigade lost direction and only a few of their men managed to enter the German defences. On their right, the West Riding Division's attack foundered and this meant that the 39th Division's infantry were now themselves exposed to enfilade fire. Ominously for Wyndham, heavy calibre German guns also began shelling the captured front line. The attack failed and, by nightfall, all the surviving troops had been withdrawn.

The 16th Rifle Brigade suffered terribly in the assault with over 400 casualties. With no-man's-land swept by fire, only a handful of riflemen managed to fight their way across and get into the German trenches. Among them was Second Lieutenant Horace Wyndham Thomas. A record exists of what happened as he gathered up the remnants of his platoon and then courageously led them into the enemy's line. A report by Private John Jones provides the sad details:

> Mr. Thomas ... was with me in the 1st line of German trenches ... when he was hit by a shell being blown to bits and killed outright. This was just as we were retiring. He had just called out "Come on, boys ... we've got them beat!" when he was hit. Then someone sang out "Retire" and we went back. I am afraid he will be posted as missing. He and I were alone together at the time. I am quite sure he was hit. He was very popular and gave all the platoon cigarettes the day before we went into action.

Some measure of the impact of his loss can be gauged by the heart-felt tributes paid to him in just a few of the very many letters of condolence received by his family. His commanding officer wrote:

> He was naturally earmarked for very early promotion, as his efficiency was remarkable ... His energy was unbounded, and he was one of those rare beings who inspire equal confidence in those above him and in those below him. I have lost a trusty officer and a friend.

Walter Durnford, the Vice-Provost of King's, was clearly distraught:

HW Thomas and LA Phillips are commemorated together on the Monmouth School War Memorial. [Gwyn Prescott]

I do not think that any death could cause such general sorrow among those who knew him as that of your son. To me personally the blow is very heavy. Wyndham was ... like an affectionate younger brother.

The college organist and choir master, Arthur Mann, wrote: "No-one that I remember during my forty years here has ever been more universally loved." The Provost of King's was M.R. James, probably best known today for his ghost stories, many of which were originally written as Christmas entertainments for friends and undergraduates, possibly including Wyndham. He told Wyndham's next of kin:

There never was surely a brighter spirit than his. I remember when we first saw him at King's ... we all said we must have him in the college. ... He ... really did ... great work for the college. Prominent as he was in the athletic world, he always did his chapel work beautifully, and made the order of clerical scholars a thing to be greatly esteemed. There are

Thiepval Memorial to the Missing of the Somme.   [Gary Williams]

few I can think of who more completely carried out their duty, gained more affection, were more missed when they went away, or more heartily welcomed when they came back to us ... ever since he kept his place in our hearts.

Horace Wyndham Thomas is commemorated on the Thiepval Memorial to the Missing of the Somme. His name can also be found next to that of his brother John, who died of wounds in 1920, on a memorial in Bettws Church. He is remembered too on memorials at Monmouth School; at the Cambridge University rugby ground in Grange Road; and in the breathtaking chapel at King's where he sang so often as an undergraduate.

There was much interest in the media in 2012 when a King's choral scholar, Rob Stephen, was selected to play full-back for Cambridge in the Varsity Match. Some speculated that he was the first King's choral scholar to become a rugby Blue but others noted it *had* been done before by Marcus Dods in 1938. But nobody seems to have called to remembrance the even greater sporting achievement of the King's choral scholar who won his Blue *and* international cap exactly a century earlier. Marcus Dods went on to have a distinguished musical career as a composer, arranger and conductor. Horace Wyndham Thomas accomplished so much in his short lifetime that we can only wonder what this exceptionally gifted young Welshman might have achieved had he survived the war.

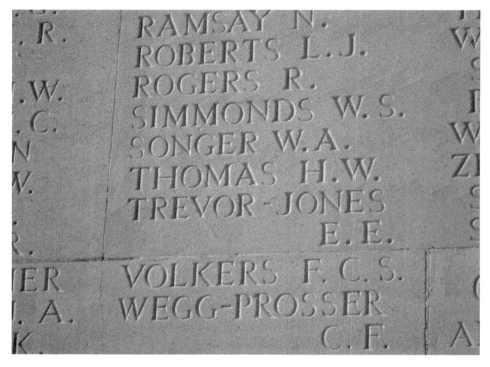

Thiepval Memorial.   [Gwyn Prescott]

William Purdon Geen

Born: Newport 14 March 1891.
Killed in action: Hooge 31 July 1915.

Teams: Haileybury College; Newport; University College, Oxford; Oxford University; Blackheath; Bridgend; Monmouthshire; Barbarians; England XV.

Wales: 3 caps, 1912-1913.

Newport-born Billy Geen was qualified to play rugby for three countries. His father was English and, while he was at Oxford, Billy had a trial for England. Through his mother, he was eligible for Ireland. He also had a strong rugby pedigree since he was the nephew of Frank Purdon, who not only played four times for Wales in the 1880s but was also rugby's first-ever, dual international. As he was Irish by birth, when Ireland arrived two men short in 1884, Purdon was one of the two local players drafted into their XV against Wales at Cardiff. Billy must have heard the story often. The Irish RFU and many others do not recognise Purdon, but Welsh match reports make it quite clear that it was indisputably Billy's uncle who represented Ireland that day. So aspirations of international rugby must have been strong and team affiliations a little blurred in the Geen household.

Easily recognised on the field with his curly fair hair, Billy was a young three-quarter from whom much was expected but who never quite realised his early promise. A player of moods, dogged by injury and occasional lapses of form, his short career was brought to a halt by the coming of war. He possessed a devastating side-step which could bewilder his opponents. The *Morning Post* recalled that "his dancing foot-work when he was striving to side-step the opposite wing was a source of intense trouble to the defence". According to Townsend Collins, at his best, he was capable of providing "dazzling entertainment" for the Rodney Parade faithful and at times even reminded older fans of Arthur Gould, unquestionably one of the greatest players of all time. He enjoyed little more than three years of senior rugby but in that time he experienced many of the highs and lows which the game can bestow.

Billy was born in 1891 into a well-to-do family who were near neighbours of Lou Phillips in Gold Tops, Newport. Like many from his social background, at an early age he was sent away to prep school and then in 1905, at the age of fourteen, Billy entered Haileybury College where he quickly gained a reputation as a sportsman. As well as representing his school at athletics and hockey, he captained the Haileybury cricket XI, playing several times for them at Lord's. While still at school, Billy kept wicket for both Newport and Monmouthshire. He first played in the Minor Counties Championship at eighteen and appeared regularly for his home county between 1909 and 1912. Generally he batted down the order but, in August 1910 when Monmouthshire required only six runs from their second innings to defeat Dorset, Billy was put in to open. He didn't let them down, confidently hitting a six to win the game. At university he played cricket for his college and also for the Oxford University Second XI.

As a member of the Haileybury XV for three years, his rugby reputation was already well established when he went up to University College, Oxford in October 1910. For the nineteen year-old, this was to be a quite a season. Regular appearances for two of the country's leading teams, Oxford Blue, county honours, Barbarians debut, English trial and Welsh reserve were all achieved in the youngster's first season of senior football.

He first came to the attention of the Welsh public in the Newport trials in September 1910 when "Old Stager" thought him the most promising of the newcomers: "Geen is well built, has a good turn of speed and an eye for an opening. Occasionally he gave glimpses of being a class player." He had several games for Newport before going up to university and no doubt the good press reviews helped with his immediate selection for the Dark Blues. Billy played at both centre and wing for Newport and Oxford, but the Welsh club tended to select him more often at centre.

Newport Athletic Club War Memorial. [Siân Prescott]

After a try-out at centre, Oxford placed him on the left wing outside Ronnie Poulton who, despite his brilliance, was regarded as a difficult centre to partner. Though Billy was also an individualist, the two developed a close understanding and they established a devastating try-scoring partnership. In 1915, only three months before Billy lost his life, Ronnie (now) "Poulton Palmer" became one of rugby's most famous war casualties when he was shot by a sniper in Belgium. Like Bryn

Lewis, Billy distinguished himself in the 1910 Varsity Match. He scored three consecutive tries in the first half, side-stepping his way through for his third. He nearly made it four, but lost the ball when over the goal-line. Even so, the Oxford victory was still in doubt until the final minutes when Poulton scored his second try to clinch the game by 23 points to 18.

After winning his first Blue, Billy took part in an English trial at Leeds, where he played for an England XV against the North, though he did not shine. Then he was selected for Monmouthshire in their 19-3 defeat of Glamorgan. Perhaps spurred into action by the interest being shown in England, the Welsh selectors retaliated by picking Billy for *their* trial in mid-January and, to strengthen their claim on him, they then named him as reserve centre and wing for the fixture with England a week later. And over Christmas, he still managed to play for Newport. Much had been expected of him at Rodney Parade following the reports of his successful partnership with Poulton but, at first, his vacation performances for the Black and Ambers were rather indifferent. However, he improved vastly in the 21-0 victory over the Barbarians, whose own selectors took note. Back at Oxford, he maintained this form, playing mostly at centre for the Varsity this term. Billy's first season then came to a rewarding climax when was he was invited to join in the fun of the Barbarians' Easter tour, playing in their fixtures at Cardiff and Cheltenham.

Despite being at Oxford, Billy had taken part in fourteen fixtures for Newport in his first season, but absence at the start of 1911-12 and a later injury meant that he was only able to play for Newport once that year. During September 1911, he was staying in the Vale of Glamorgan, so instead of travelling home to play, he temporarily joined Bridgend and had several games there alongside Dick Thomas. He made the most of this time at Bridgend and was increasingly talked about as a future international. The press argued his case even more strongly when he returned to Oxford. After the Dark Blues despatched Gloucester 18-0, "Old Stager" thought he was now a serious prospect for the Welsh wing. An invitation to play for the Probables in the trial followed but he was unable to accept because of university commitments. Undaunted by his unavailability though, the Welsh selectors decided to attend the 1911 Varsity Match to check on Billy's form, as well as that of Bryn Lewis of Cambridge. Billy had suffered the odd lapse for Oxford that season but he rose to the occasion on the big day, though he did manage to repeat his trick of crossing the line and failing to score. Cambridge were favourites, but they had been forced to replace the injured Wyndham Thomas at the last minute, and Oxford eventually ran out winners by 19 points to nil.

Billy was then selected again by the Barbarians, this time for their

Possibles XV 1910-11. Back: CM Pritchard, WP Geen, A Coldrick, T Morgan, J Birch, PL Jones, - Stephens?, E Marsh; Front: W Martin, F Rees, E Mithan, T Vile, F Birt, E Davies, BR Lewis. [WRU]

Christmas tour. Unfortunately, though, this led to a major setback for his career. In the Boxing Day game against Cardiff, which was lost 19-0, he sustained a serious injury which required surgery. This not only ruled out any possibility of his winning his Welsh cap that year but it also put paid to the rest of his season.

So there was some concern at Oxford that Billy would not be available for the 1912 Varsity Match but he dispelled all such fears when, in early October, he proved his fitness by playing on the wing for Newport in two big games against Cardiff and Blackheath. He again hit top form for the Dark Blues and the Welsh selectors were surely delighted to read in the English press that "Geen must be one of the most difficult men to tackle"; that he "did wonders with the little elbow room allowed him"; and, in particular, that he was "playing as well as ever". On 23 October, he scored four tries from the wing in Oxford's 24-0 victory over London Hospital. Even in 1912 this was not the strongest of fixtures but the very next day Billy found himself unexpectedly pitched into a contest against far sterner opponents. Fortuitously for him, Newport's meeting with the Springboks was scheduled for a Thursday so, when a late replacement was required,

Billy was able to respond to a call for help from his home club. This would turn out be one of the highlights of his short career. In one of the most memorable games in the club's history, Newport deservedly won a fast and exciting game by 9 points to 3. It was a strenuous struggle in which the home forwards got the better of the tourists. Praised for his fine tackling, Billy played his part in the heroic defence by the Newport backs and saved at least one certain try. Naturally, the 20,000 crowd were delirious at the first defeat of the 1912 Springboks but there was little time for celebration for Billy, who had to return to Oxford for his third game in four days against Richmond. Shortly afterwards, he was facing South Africa again, when he had one of his best games that season for the university. This time he was on the losing side by 6 points to 0 but again he demonstrated that he could defend as well as attack. "Time after time, W.A. Krige got the ball and either dropped it or fell easy prey to the speedy Geen", *The Times* noted.

Billy was unable to make it three out of three in the 1912 Varsity Match when Cambridge thoroughly deserved their first win since 1905. In another good performance, however, he was, according to *The Times*, "a source of much trouble" to the Light Blues even though the timing of his centre's passing was so poor that, when Billy received the ball, he was usually faced by three opponents. "Two of these he would normally dodge, for he was in splendid form, but the third was too much for him." Alas, for the third year running, he lost the ball while in the act of scoring. Nevertheless, the *Western Mail* judged him a success and the Welsh selectors, who were in attendance to check on Wyndham Thomas, were delighted that Billy had justified their decision of a few days earlier to award Billy his first Welsh cap.

Billy was one of nine Welshmen making their international debut against South Africa, so it was an inexperienced side which took the field at Cardiff. The conditions were dreadful. Heavy rain had turned the pitch into a sea of mud and a gale-force wind made handling extremely difficult and both sides missed several try-scoring opportunities. This was a game which Wales might have won and, with South Africa hanging on to a slim 3-0 lead, there was always a possibility of a break-away score. Billy looked as though he might be the man to do it when in the second half he sensationally ran the length of the field and, with only the full-back to beat, he chipped over his head but agonisingly just missed touching down by inches as the ball slithered into touch-in-goal. This was just one of several swerving runs he made and he certainly impressed at least one South African correspondent: "Geen, a grand defender, a determined runner, the best wing on the field, need never wish to play a finer game."

Billy Geen on his debut for Wales.

Back home on vacation, he squeezed in five matches for the Black and Ambers as well as another game for the Barbarians when he partnered Edgar Mobbs at centre and scored a try in a 15-11 defeat at Leicester. There was never any doubt that he would keep his place for the visit of England to Cardiff on 18 January 1913 and he must have gone into the match with some confidence. However, England ran out comfortable winners by 12 points to 0 to record their first ever victory at the Arms Park. Although Wales were outplayed behind, Billy managed to make a few openings and was the most dangerous player in the home side. During the second half, the majority of the English attacks were directed towards his wing but he coped with them well. "Time after time he pluckily fielded and extricated himself from ugly situations." Without him, therefore, the defeat might easily have been worse.

Billy was selected for the Edinburgh international a fortnight later but cried off. The press reported that he was indisposed. Then he pulled out of the French match a month later. This time it was said that he had sustained an injury playing against England, though he had played for Oxford after this game. "Sport was probably the subject he read most thoroughly" according to one commentator on his time at Oxford, so perhaps for once working on his law studies had to take priority. Whatever the reason for his absence, he was back in the Welsh XV for the season's final match against Ireland at Swansea and it must have been a memorable experience for him.

This time there was to be a change, however. Many in Wales had always believed that he had greater potential at centre rather than wing and the selectors now decided to test this. Wales had defeated both Scotland and France and were expected to gain a straightforward victory over a demoralised Irish XV, but in the end they just scraped home by 16 points to 13. It was a pulsating match though, "one of the most exhilarating ever played." On a perfect St. Helens pitch, Billy more than vindicated the selectors' confidence in him and was a great success at centre, making many breaks and swerving runs and timing his passes perfectly. A week later, after Newport defeated their old rivals Cardiff by 23 points to 10, "Old Stager" – a Cardiff journalist after all – wrote that Billy had an outstanding game, adding that he had the potential to become a great centre. Comparisons with Rhys Gabe were being made. Much was now expected of him.

Regrettably, Billy never lived up to these expectations and his last season was a very disappointing one in which he was only regularly seen in Newport colours for a few weeks between November and January. In his second game, he was involved in an ugly incident at Neath which he must have found very disturbing. Newport lost 11-6 despite Billy's two tries but, towards the end of the match, a Neath player was knocked unconscious in a tackle and Billy was alleged to have kicked him. He was subjected to a very hostile reaction from the crowd and, as he left the field at the end of the game, he was physically attacked by some of the Gnoll supporters. There followed more controversy, though this time less serious, when he was involved in yet another missed try – his fourth – against Cambridge. As Billy crossed the line to score, the Cambridge touch-judge raised his flag in excitement. Although he immediately admitted that Billy had not put his foot in touch, the referee determined that, since the touch-judge *had* raised his flag, he had to award the line-out. As they lost the match 13-10, Newport were *not* impressed with the referee's pedantry. Although Billy was not quite showing the form of the previous season, he was still picked at centre for the England match at Twickenham. Then, on the Saturday before the international, in what turned out to be his last game for the club, he played in Newport's 5-3 defeat at Penarth. "Forward" commented on his performance, "Geen did not come into the picture at all". The *Evening Express* reported that he had been out of condition for a while and probably should not have been playing. Something was wrong. A few days later it was announced that, on medical advice, he was unable to play against England. The *South Wales Daily News* reported that Billy's message to the WRU did not disclose the nature of any injury or how it had occurred, perhaps hinting at some irritation or even scepticism. Whatever the circumstances, he played no more senior rugby in Wales in 1913-14 and the absence of a fit Billy Geen from Twickenham may have been costly, as his replacement made a crucial error which presented England with both victory and, as it turned out, the Grand Slam.

When war broke out, Billy was amongst the very first to volunteer. He had been a cadet in the Officer Training Corps at Haileybury and so was immediately commissioned second lieutenant in August 1914 and he joined the 9th (Service) Battalion The King's Royal Rifle Corps which was then forming in Winchester. One of the first Kitchener battalions to be raised during the war, the 9th KRRC moved to Aldershot where they came under orders of the 42nd Brigade, 14th (Light) Division. The title of "Light" Division was conferred because all the original battalions came from rifle

Newport Athletic Club War Memorial gates. [Siân Prescott]

and light infantry regiments. Three months later, the 9th KRRC moved to Petworth, Sussex, where they went into billets; and they returned to Aldershot the following February for final Divisional training before going overseas. While based there, Billy was invited by the Barbarians to take part in what turned out to be his last game of rugby. In an entertaining match at Old Deer Park on 10 April 1915, he helped the Barbarians defeat the Royal Army Medical Corps 10-3. Partnering him in the three-quarters that day were Edgar Mobbs and, another English international fated to die in the war, Arthur Dingle. A week before this match, Billy had been expected to play for the Welsh XV against the Barbarians but his military duties had prevented him travelling to Cardiff where his services were sorely missed. Only a little over three months after these events, he too he would give his life for his country.

On 20 May 1915, Billy disembarked at Boulogne with his battalion. After a few weeks acclimatisation, in the middle of June, the 14th (Light) Division took over trenches in the Salient, about two miles east of Ypres, around the village and chateau of Hooge. This was not a quiet sector. There was constant shelling, the area was hotly contested by the enemy and it was subjected to what the regimental history describes as "considerable bickering". The hostility became far more intense, however, on the morning of 30 July when the Germans launched a fierce attack on the part of the line at Hooge held by a sister brigade in the Light Division, the 41st Brigade. Suddenly at 3.15 in the morning, jets of flame burst across the front line trenches and the ill-fated 41st found themselves facing the first ever use of liquid fire against British troops. At the same time, the Germans opened up with every other kind of fire: high explosive shells, trench mortars, hand grenades, machine guns and shrapnel all swept the front line and the open ground behind. The surprise was complete and the 41st Brigade's front trenches were then overwhelmed and captured by the enemy.

While this was happening, Billy's 42nd Brigade, on the left, had been largely unaffected by the horrific offensive. The 9th KRRC were not even in the line at the time, having been in reserve for several days, but they were now rushed up to support their hard-pressed comrades. A new line was consolidated and, despite the request of the Brigadier-General for more re-enforcements, at 2.15 p.m. a counter-attack was hastily mounted by the survivors of the 41st Brigade, assisted by the 9th KRRC, to try to recover the lost ground. However, in the words of the Official History, the preliminary artillery bombardment was feeble in comparison with that of the earlier German onslaught. As the Brigadier-General, the man on the ground, had feared, the inadequately prepared counter-attack stood little chance of success.

The troops of the already battered and jaded 41st Division failed to get near their objectives, though it was a different story for the better-rested men of the 9th KRRC who were able to retake part of the trenches near the Menin Road which had been lost that morning. During their re-capture, the leading riflemen had come under raking fire from Hooge village. So with his blood up, Second Lieutenant Geen courageously responded by taking it upon himself to lead a small party forward and close with the enemy. But it seems Billy's dodging skills were not enough this time. He was never seen again.

The 9th Battalion The King's Royal Rifle Corps lost nearly 350 killed, wounded or missing during this action. Billy was initially reported missing and this may explain why his date of death in all the records is given as the day after the counter-attack. Yet another player whose best years were robbed by the war, the

Ypres (Menin Gate) Memorial to the Missing.   [Gary Williams]

gallant Billy Geen is one of seven rugby internationals, and over 54,000 others, whose names are commemorated on the Ypres (Menin Gate) Memorial to the Missing of the Salient.[1]

As well as William Geen, the KRRC panel on the Menin Gate also commemorates the English international, RO Lagden, who played for Oxford with him in two Varsity Matches. [britishcemeteries.webs.com]

---

1 The other internationals are: James Henderson, James Ross (Scotland); Ronald Lagden, Edgar Mobbs, Arthur Wilson (England); and Basil Maclear (Ireland).

Fred Leonard Perrett

Born: Briton Ferry 9 May 1891.
Died of wounds: Boulogne 1 December 1918.

Teams: Briton Ferry; Aberavon; Neath; Glamorgan.

Wales: 5 caps, 1912-1913.

Mortally wounded in the last week of the Great War, for a long time Fred Perrett was omitted from lists of rugby internationals who made the supreme sacrifice. It is now a widespread belief that he was deliberately excluded because he became a Northern Union professional in 1913. Within months of the war ending, Edward Sewell published his *Rugby Football Internationals' Roll of Honour,* containing biographies of some eighty-nine players who fell. Fred Perrett was not amongst them. The book is a fine tribute to these men but, as Sewell was writing so soon after the war, he was not able to include every international player. Over 130 actually lost their lives. Therefore, it was never a *definitive* roll of honour, though it was widely accepted as such for many years.

As a journalist of the English rugby establishment, Sewell might have been expected to omit Fred because he had joined the professional code. However, Sewell clearly had no prejudice against professionals in this matter because he *included* the English forward, William Nanson, who joined the Northern Union. Besides, Fred Perrett wasn't the only Welshman to be left out, as Dai Watts, who did not turn professional, is not in Sewell's roll either.

As it was the only comprehensive source of its kind, later writers referring to rugby and the Great War naturally turned to Sewell. This is why the names of Fred Perrett and Dai Watts were not included alongside those of the other eleven Welsh internationals in the WRU Official History published

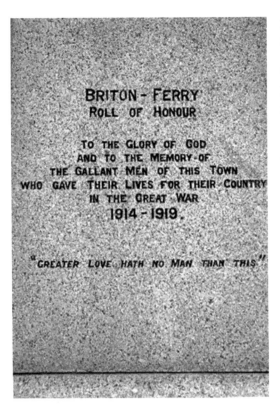

Briton Ferry War Memorial.   [Siân Prescott]

in 1981. Even today, references to eleven rather than thirteen are still made.

Furthermore, the suggestion that the WRU deliberately conspired to exclude Fred Perrett because he had "gone north" is hard to credit when it is remembered that, after the war, the Union argued for the reinstatement of all professionals who had served in the war, though they were unable to persuade the RFU about this. A conspiracy against Fred Perrett's inclusion makes a good story and it may well remain the accepted version, but the most likely explanation is that, as with Dai Watts, his exclusion from the roll of honour was simply an oversight.

Fred Perrett was born in 1891 in Briton Ferry, the small industrial town on the banks of the river Neath, where his father was a ship's pilot. He was educated at the local National School and was employed initially as a steelworker. His first club was Briton Ferry and by 1910-11, the twenty year-old was already impressing local journalists and club officials on the look-out for promising talent. Before that season was over, he had joined Aberavon and he would have come to the notice of the Neath committee in February 1911 when he and his fellow forwards out-scrummaged the Neath pack, despite losing 10-0.

He remained with Aberavon for the next season and continued to mature. Fred must have been thrilled to read press match reports now regularly referring to him as one of the best forwards on the field, even in Aberavon's matches with the likes of Swansea and Llanelli. This surely fuelled his ambition. At the end of 1911-12, he was selected for a Rest of Wales XV and even though this was only a low-key charity match, it is an indication that he was already becoming recognised as a young player of some potential.

After two highly successful years in which they had won and retained the Welsh Championship, Neath's 1911-12 season did not quite reach the same heights. So they would have been delighted to recruit the up-and-coming young forward for the 1912-13 campaign. And it was to be a spectacular season for Fred. It began with a comprehensive 24-0 victory in the opening fixture at the Gnoll against the tough Monmouthshire League side Pill Harriers. A series of consistent displays for his new club led to his selection two months later for Glamorgan. Despite losing 8-0 to Monmouthshire in front of a derisory mid-week crowd at the Arms Park (county rugby has never excited the Welsh public), Fred had demonstrated enough for the selectors to include him in the Welsh trial held on 5 December 1912, nine days before the South African international. As so often happened, the trial was not a great success and only seven of the participants were selected for Wales. But amongst them was the twenty-one year-old Fred Perrett, whose rise to the very pinnacle of the sport had been swift. He was one of six new caps at forward, but "Old Stager" was optimistic about them all: "There is not a man among the eight who is not distinguished by pluck, all are resolute tacklers and every one is a hard grafter."

Nevertheless, despite the efforts of Fred Perrett, Billy Geen and Wyndham Thomas, Wales suffered their first defeat in Cardiff since 1899, as they went down narrowly to the South Africans by a single penalty goal to nil. The Springboks' captain, Billy Millar, admitted that it was the hardest game he had ever played in. Though they were outpaced by their heavier opponents, the new Welsh pack did well enough and Fred was praised for his "good work". In a fast and keenly contested match, the Welsh forwards managed to remain competitive throughout, so all eight were re-selected for the forthcoming game with England.

Before then, however, Fred had to face the Springboks again, appearing this time for his club. In 1908-9, Neath had combined with Aberavon to meet the Australian tourists but, in recognition of their later successes, they were now deservedly awarded a prestigious fixture against the South Africans in their own right. Played five days after the Wales match, Neath were expected to give the visitors a tough time and they did, coming desperately close to pulling off an historic victory. The forwards tackled well and were dominant in the loose. *The Times* described them as "masters of the art of close dribble" which the Springbok backs struggled to counter. Glyn Stephens, T.C Lloyd and Fred Perrett were "the best of a very good eight, who fully justified their reputation". The Welsh press were also complimentary about Fred's play. Though they lost 8-3, it was a moral victory for Neath, particularly as T.C. Lloyd had a try controversially disallowed.

Fred's next big match was in January 1913 against England at Cardiff. This was a tremendous battle up front but the English eight were faster and better organised. The Welsh backs were outclassed and, with "Cherry" Pillman seemingly at the head of every forward attack, England won by two tries, one conversion and a drop goal to nil and they subsequently went on to record their first Grand Slam. After this poor performance, the Welsh selectors rang the changes dramatically and only five players, Fred Perrett amongst them, were judged worthy of retention for Edinburgh. One of the new caps was the Reverend Alban Davies who was to lead Wales with such success the following season. The reconstituted pack not only out-scrummaged Scotland they also beat them at their own traditional "foot rushing" game. A strong wind and bitter cold made passing difficult but the backs still managed two tries to give Wales an 8-0 victory.[1] One of these was an opportunistic effort by JMC "Clem" Lewis, who proved to be a successful replacement for the India-bound Wyndham Thomas at outside-half. Serving as a captain in the Cardiff City Battalion during the war, Clem was wounded in the Battle of Pilckem Ridge in 1917 but still became one of the few men to play varsity and international rugby both before and after the war.

Three weeks later Wales travelled to Paris. They had beaten France in their previous five encounters, but this match proved to be the closest so far. The French were quick on the ball and tackled ferociously. The sides were level for much of the second half and only after some determined attacking did Wales manage to snatch an 11-8 victory in the last few minutes with a Clem Lewis try. Opposing Fred in the pack was Maurice Boyau, who became one of France's most successful fighter pilots of the war. He was killed in September 1918 and today his statue stands outside the rugby stadium in Dax which is named after him. Following serious crowd disturbances in the previous match against Scotland at Parc des Princes, there was a heavy police presence for the visit of Wales. Perhaps anticipating more trouble, towards the end of the game a squadron of mounted Republican Guard took up position on the Welsh goal-line, evidently unaware that they were on the field of play. They were eventually moved off by the referee and officials amid ironic cheers from the crowd. As it happens, there was no trouble at the end and not only were Wales given a standing ovation but the referee was carried off on the shoulders of the spectators.

There now only remained the Irish match at Swansea in March, in which Billy Geen and Bryn Lewis also took part. This turned out to be one the finest ever witnessed at St. Helens. Ireland were expected to be despatched easily but their forwards defied all predictions and performed brilliantly in

---

1   Shockingly, the Scottish XV in this match suffered ten fatalities in the war. They were: Cecil Abercrombie, David Bain, Patrick Blair, Walter Dickson, Rowland Gordon, David Howie, Eric Milroy, Lewis Robertson, Walter Sutherland and Frederic Turner.

Wales v Ireland 1913. Back: F Andrews, FL Perrett, WP Geen, TC Lloyd, R Richards, Alban Davies, G Stephens; Middle: WJ Jenkins, H Uzzell, JP Jones, J Bancroft, H Lewis, BR Lewis; Front: JMC Lewis, R Lloyd.   [WRU]

open play. The Welsh pack, however, concentrated on doing the basics well and they provided plenty of good ball for the backs from the set pieces. Billy, Bryn and Fred were all in great form and Wales eventually ran out winners by 16-13, confirming their runners-up position in the 1912-13 Championship table.

It had been an extraordinary season for Fred but personal circumstances now intervened to take his blossoming rugby career in an entirely different direction. For a hundred years from the formation of the Northern Union in 1895 to the professionalisation of rugby union, huge numbers of talented Welsh players were lost by "going north" and it is impossible to estimate the damage this did to the domestic game and the national team over the years. One such loss was Fred Perrett. He had previously rejected approaches from Bramley and Hunslet scouts but when, in the May following the Irish international, he found himself out of work, he was unable to resist the generous terms offered by Leeds. The subsequent treatment of great servants to the game like Fred, for whom turning professional offered some financial security, is a deeply shameful episode in the history of rugby union.

The local press claimed that Fred's signing-on fee was the largest ever paid to a forward. Newspapers were no more reliable then than they are today in reporting such matters but it may perhaps provide an indication of

Briton Ferry War Memorial.   [Siân Prescott]

the level of interest which the professional game had in him. At the end of the month, he headed for Yorkshire where he had been found employment with a car manufacturing firm. Fred made his debut for Leeds against Broughton Rangers on 6 September 1913. After his first professional season, in April 1914 he transferred to Hull, his fifth club in as many years. Here he was given a job in a shipyard, working as a plater's helper. Despite the outbreak of war, the Northern Union decided to carry on more or less as usual in 1914-15 and Hull completed a full programme of fixtures that season, finishing fifth in the Championship. Fred saw the season out before answering the call to arms – his fellow Welsh international Len Trump had to return part of his signing-on fee to Hull Kingston Rovers when he joined the Army during contract – but once released by Hull, Fred enlisted in the Welsh Guards on 20 July 1915.

The Welsh Guards were the only new infantry regiment to be raised during the Great War. They began forming in February 1915 and on St. David's Day stood their first guard duty over the King. By August, the 1st Battalion was in France. Before Fred went out, however, he had to undergo training with the 2nd (Reserve) Battalion, which spent the autumn at Marlow and the winter at the Tower of London, where one of their responsibilities was to guard captured German spies. There may have been some rugby for Fred too, since, during wartime, restrictions on the participation of professionals were lifted. By the end of the war, the Welsh Guards had acquired such a reputation for rough play that the London Society of Referees refused to officiate in their matches. Perhaps they were winning too often.

Training at last completed, Fred was one of a draft of 110 guardsmen who joined the 1st Battalion at Calais in late February 1916. Between then and August, the Guards Division were in the Ypres Salient holding the Bellewaarde and Wieltje sector. The Welsh Guards went into the line there on the 20 March and Fred's war now began for real. The trenches were a quagmire and even though his battalion were not involved in any attacks between April and June, they still suffered 115 casualties in the day-to-day attrition of trench life. Up till then, they had only engaged in patrolling against the enemy, but on 1 July, the Welsh Guards carried out an attack on an enemy position near Wieltje known as "Mortaldje Estaminet" though it was some time since anyone had bought a drink there as it now comprised only a pile of bricks and girders. Yet its capture and consolidation cost the battalion another ninety-six casualties. Shortly afterwards, Fred was appointed Lance Corporal, and then the Guards left the villainous Salient to take over trenches on the Somme in August. On the night of 9 September they relieved the exhausted men of the 16th (Irish) Division who had just successfully captured the shattered remains of Ginchy. The Germans made several fierce attempts to re-capture the village but these were fought off in brutal hand-to-hand fighting in which the Welsh Guards suffered 205 casualties. In the next couple of weeks, they again distinguished themselves in the Battle of Flers-Courcellette, when Fred may have had his first glimpse of tanks in action, and in the Battle of Morval, though a further 223 casualties were incurred.

Taking part in all this desperate and blood-soaked fighting at Ypres and the Somme, Fred had impressed his superiors and so he was then recommended for a commission by his commanding officer. A few days before Christmas 1916, he left the carnage behind for a while to receive officer training in Britain. This included four months with an Officer Cadet Battalion in Bristol, where emphasis was placed on instilling leadership, initiative and self-confidence in prospective officers, many of whom, like Fred, had come up from the ranks. Successfully completing the course, he was commissioned with effect from 27 June 1917 in the 3rd (Reserve) Battalion The Royal Welsh Fusiliers, who were based at Litherland, near Liverpool. After spending some leave with his family, he returned to the Western Front and on 2 October 1917 joined the 17th (Service) Battalion (2nd North Wales) The Royal Welsh Fusiliers. This unit had originally been raised in February 1915 at Llandudno and five months later they came under the orders of the 115th Brigade, 38th (Welsh) Division. In the autumn of 1917, they were now in reserve recovering from the slaughter of Third Ypres in the "comparative quiet" of the Armentières area. Going into the line at nearby Houplines, a few days after arriving, was hardly a pleasant re-introduction to trench life for Fred. The area was low-lying and water-logged, and working parties, night patrols and raids were regular events. He had, however, experienced it all before.

The Welsh Division didn't participate in any large-scale battles again until the Second Battle of the Somme of August-September 1918. However, the reality of warfare on the Western Front meant that the attrition in lives continued remorselessly. Fred himself became a casualty at Bouzincourt on the Somme in April 1918 when he received a slight gunshot wound to his

Briton Ferry War Memorial. [Siân Prescott]

shoulder and was hospitalised in Rouen for a short while. However, after the failure of the major German offences of 1918, the enemy now fell back towards their formidable defensive system, the Hindenburg Line. During September and early October, Fred was regularly in action as the Welsh Division fought at the Battles of Havrincourt, Épehy, Beaurevoir Line and Cambrai. This was now the "Last 100 Days", a period of astonishing and unprecedented success for British and Commonwealth forces, yet one often ignored by posterity. By 5 October, the Allies had the whole of the Hindenburg Line in their hands and the war was now effectively over but the Germans continued to resist. In the "Final Advance to Victory" the Welsh Division participated in the Battle of the Selle in late October when the enemy's new defensive position on the river was overcome. Fred had managed to come through all this bloodshed largely unscathed. But there was to be one final engagement for the 17th RWF and for Fred: the Battle of the Sambre.

On the 26 October, the 38th Division had reached Englefontaine and were now confronted by Mormal Forest, the largest wood in this part of France. The Germans were expected to defend it strongly, so the attack was delayed to allow time for adequate preparation. Three objectives were identified. The first was a line about 500 yards from the western edge of the forest. Designated the "Blue Line", this was to be captured by Fred's 115th Brigade, comprising the 17th RWF, 2nd RWF and 10th South Wales Borderers. Once this was taken, the 113th Brigade, which had been following up, would leapfrog the 115th and move on to the next objective the "Red Line". Then, in their turn, the 114th Brigade would pass through the 113th Brigade and advance onto the final objective, the "Green Line". All went according to plan. Zero hour was 6.15 a.m. on 4 November. The leading brigade, the 115th met the strongest resistance since the defenders were well dug in at the edge of the forest. There were also many open spaces within the wood, which gave the Germans a good field of fire as the attackers drove in; while several very strongly-fenced orchards also threatened to slow the momentum of the attack. Despite losing a good number of men, the Welsh troops doggedly pressed on and reached their objective. Enemy resistance then collapsed and, as planned, the 113th Brigade passed through the Blue Line meeting little opposition. The 114th Brigade then took the

Terlincthun British Cemetery, Wimille, Boulogne. [The War Graves Photographic Project]

final Green Line and pushed on through the night beyond the wood, even capturing the first objective of the next day's attack. It had been a highly successful final battle for the 38th (Welsh) Division but, as always, there was a heavy price to pay.

Just as the brigades had leapfrogged each other in the attack, so too did the individual battalions in each brigade. The 17th RWF were tasked with the final leg of the assault on the Blue Line. Eight members of the battalion were killed during the capture of Mormal Forest and forty-four were wounded. This was the last occasion the 17th Royal Welsh Fusiliers went into action.

Bravely leading his men in the attack, Second Lieutenant Perrett was severely wounded in his left hand and right thigh, probably by machine-gun fire. It was exactly a week before the Armistice and, on this same day, in another part of the Battle of the Sambre, the poet, Wilfred Owen, was killed at Ors in the crossing of the Sambre-Oise canal. Fred was stretchered out of the wood and taken to an aid post where he received basic treatment. Then he was carried via a chain of medical posts to a casualty clearing station, where his condition was assessed and stabilised as best as possible. From there he was despatched by rail to a base hospital on the French coast. Four days after the battle, on 8 November, he arrived at No 8 British Red Cross Hospital

Fred Leonard Perrett's headstone at Terlincthun.   [The War Graves Photographic Project]

at Boulogne. A week later, his wife was advised by telegram that he was dangerously ill and, ominously, that she had permission to travel to Boulogne to visit him. Tragically, his condition continued to deteriorate and he died of a secondary haemorrhage on 1 December 1918, leaving his grieving widow to bring up their two young sons alone. He is buried in the Terlincthun British Cemetery at Wimille on the northern outskirts of Boulogne. This contains over 5,000 First World War burials, the majority of which are of those who died in base hospitals in the area.

Whatever the reason for Fred Perrett's heroic sacrifice being overlooked in the past, he now takes his rightful place of honour alongside his fellow Welsh internationals on the WRU's memorial plaque at the Millennium Stadium.

David Watts

Born: Cwmdu, Maesteg 14 March 1886.
Killed in action:, Bazentin Ridge 14 July 1916.

Teams: Maesteg Quins; Aberaman; Merthyr; Rhymney; Maesteg; Bridgend; Glamorgan League; Glamorgan

Wales: 4 caps, 1914.

T he Commonwealth War Graves Commission's imposing Memorial to the Missing dominates the skyline for many miles around Thiepval. It was dedicated to commemorate over 72,000 British and South Africans, who died on the Somme before 20 March 1918 and who have no known grave. It will therefore take a little time finding them, but the names of nine rugby internationals are recorded there. However, one of the most difficult to locate – because it is high up on the memorial panels – is that of D. Watts of The King's (Shropshire Light Infantry).[1] Over the thirty-three years up to the Great War, Wales played 102 international matches. Richard Davies Garnons Williams was in the first ever Welsh line-up in 1881: the very last pre-war international XV also included a victim of the war. That player was David Watts.

While RDG Williams became a country landowner, "Dai" Watts was a member of a mining family. He was born in Cwmdu, Maesteg in 1886, and must have had a very hard early life because his mother had to bring him up alone after his father left them and went to America. Like so many others of his background, by the time he was sixteen, he was already working underground at the coal-face as a hewer, probably at the local village colliery.

---

1   The others are: Rowland Fraser and Eric Milroy (Scotland); Rupert Inglis, John King, Alfred Maynard and L. Andrew Slocock (England); and H. Wyndham Thomas and Richard Thomas (Wales).

Thiepval Memorial to the Missing of the Somme.   [Gary Williams]

He began his career with Maesteg Quins, but later joined a variety of valley clubs. This may have been because he was following work or perhaps he was offered financial inducements to move. It was a common practice of many Welsh clubs at the time to ignore rugby union's strict amateur regulations and make payments to players and/or find them employment. The sums were generally not large but nevertheless they could make a more than welcome addition to a miner's income. There is no evidence that Dai received any "boot money" but whatever the circumstances, he played for both Aberaman and Merthyr in the Glamorgan League. This had been established in 1894-5 to provide good competition for ambitious valley clubs just outside the top flight. League matches could attract large crowds and they generated enormous enthusiasm, though the intensity of feeling sometimes spilled over onto the pitch. This was a playing environment in which you had to be tough to thrive and it was one which undoubtedly prepared Dai well for his later international career. By 1908 when playing for Merthyr, he had already acquired some reputation at this level as he was selected to represent North Glamorgan in an unofficial fixture against the Australian touring team, though he was unable to play.

By 1911 he had moved to Aberbargoed with his wife and young son and was now representing Rhymney in the equally competitive Monmouthshire League. However, in 1912 he returned to his home town and joined Maesteg. Founded as early as October 1877, by the First World War they had become a very successful club. With Dai's help, they confirmed their status as one of the top teams outside the leading

Maesteg War Memorial. A scroll bearing the names of Maesteg's war dead was sealed in a chamber within the memorial.   [Siân Prescott]

elite by winning the 1912-13 Glamorgan League title, effectively the second division of Welsh rugby. They had never previously had a player capped directly from the club, but that was soon to change. During the first few months of 1913-14, Maesteg defeated teams of the calibre of Bridgend, Cross Keys, Pontypridd and London Irish and it was these and other successes which brought Dai to the attention of the Welsh selectors. He was already acknowledged as one of the best and toughest forwards in the Glamorgan League but his reputation would soon reach a very much wider audience. It is no exaggeration to say that Dai shot to prominence in a very short time. In October 1913, he represented the Glamorgan League in their no-holds-barred annual derby with the Monmouthshire League and, following an excellent display, he was then selected for the Glamorgan County XV against both Monmouthshire and Devon. On the winning side in all three matches, his impressive performances at representative level then resulted in his inclusion in the Welsh trial.

When the team was announced for the first international in 1914 against England, there was, as is not unknown in Wales, controversy. Some questions were raised about Dai's selection because, not playing for a senior club, he was relatively unknown. But his detractors underestimated him. He was immensely strong and, at five foot eleven (1.80m) and fourteen stone two pounds (89.8kg), was solidly built. And he was to become a cornerstone of one of the most famous – some might say infamous – and fearsome packs ever put in the field by Wales.

The first game at Twickenham proved to be the decisive contest of the season and the whole outcome of the Championship turned on one crucial error committed eight minutes from time. There may have been some concern amongst the large crowds seeing the team off at Cardiff station when they learned that Billy Geen, who had played so well in the previous season's fixture, had pulled out and had been replaced by the inexperienced Llanelli centre Willie Watts (no relation). But "Old Stager" still found reason to be confident, noting that the players were taking the match "with an earnestness that has seldom been exceeded by a Welsh team since the eve of the memorable victory over New Zealand."

The newspapers claimed that the match receipts at Twickenham broke all rugby records with the takings from the 30,000 crowd amounting to £4,100. It was even breathlessly reported that no fewer than 150 cars had parked at the ground and that their owners had paid two shillings each for the privilege. Whether they brought hampers with them was not recorded. The match lived up to expectations. *The Times* thought it was the best of the ten internationals so far witnessed at Twickenham. This was definitely a game that Wales should have won. The Welsh pack trounced their opposition, as *The Times* admitted: "the English forwards were beaten. They had against them eight men of splendid physique in perfect training, man for man heavier and stronger. These Welshmen knew every move of forward play." The *Cardiff Times* agreed: "The Welsh forwards excelled themselves ... beating their belauded opponents in heeling, rushing and in general play." So in helping to overwhelm the cream of English talent, Dai was able to demonstrate once and for all, to any critics, that playing all his rugby for "unfashionable" valley clubs was no drawback.

But you only win matches by scoring more points than your opponents. Although the Welsh pack and half-backs were outstanding, Wales were badly let down behind. It was the weakest attacking three-quarter line Wales had fielded in fifteen years, according to *The Times*. The forwards gave them plenty of chances but they failed to make any progress. Their alignment was poor, they impeded each other and they dropped passes. To make matters worse, opposite them at centre was the matchless Ronnie Poulton and he was on great form. Even so, Wales got off to a good start. Outside-half Clem Lewis was held up on the line twice but then winger George Hirst dropped a magnificent goal from the touchline. England hit back though when Poulton brilliantly exposed the weakness at centre and created a try which was converted. They now led 5-4. In the second half, Jack Bancroft missed two penalties before Willie Watts charged down a Poulton kick, gathered and scored. Bancroft was successful this time and Wales were back in the lead 9-5. With the forwards well on top, victory now seemed well within Wales's grasp. An awkward bounce just prevented winger Howell Lewis from scoring, which would have put the game out of England's reach. Then, with less than ten minutes left, during a rare English incursion into the Welsh half, a nervy Willie Watts fumbled the ball near the goal-line and inexplicably froze. The scourge of earlier encounters, "Cherry" Pillman, pounced on the loose ball and scored under the posts. The conversion was successful and England managed to hold on desperately to win 10-9. Wales had not only fumbled the match but, as it turned out, they had fumbled the Triple Crown and Grand Slam too.

It must have been with very mixed feelings that Dai read the press reports. After all, the forwards had done so well. *The Referee* told its readers: "the Welshmen should have won and deserved to do so ... the English forwards were a rabble". According to the *Sunday Times*, it was "a very lucky win ... Wales had three-fourths, if not more, of the play ... Wales ... have scarcely ever commanded as great a pack as that which took the field on Saturday." It was left to *The Times* to sum it up: "Wales, the better team on the day, retired beaten by fate and Poulton." As the Irish forwards read about the match, they may have particularly taken note of another comment in *The*

Wales v Scotland 1914. Back: PL Jones, TC Lloyd, E Morgan, (Referee), D Watts, H Uzzell, TB Jones; Middle: IT Davies, JMC Lewis, J Bancroft, Alban Davies, G Hirst, JJ Wetter, T Williams; Front: WH Evans, R Lloyd.   [WRU]

Times: "It was no child's play in the loose scrimmage, quarter was unasked and ungiven."

Despite the inevitable post-match disappointment, the way the forwards played must have given them great heart for the rest of the season. With a strengthened three-quarter line, Wales forcefully despatched Scotland 24-5 at Cardiff. The pack were again dominant. "The intuition of the Welsh forwards was superb ... they laid the foundations of a glorious victory", the *Glasgow Herald* acknowledged. Some press reports may have had the Irish licking their lips with anticipation again. *The Times* thought that "there was a little too much wild play, an excess of patriotism in the loose scrimmages." Evidently some of the rucking had been over-keen. After the match, the Scottish captain, David Bain, with six stitches in his head, complained that the dirtier team had won. The Welsh captain Reverend Alban Davies responded nonchalantly, "play was very keen ... but we Welsh players take this in good part ... we had more men badly hurt than the Scotch ... the Scots were none too gentle". For good measure, he added that he was covered in bruises. Alban Davies survived the war as a chaplain in the 38th (Welsh) Division but sadly David Bain and three of his team-mates lost their lives.

France had pushed Wales somewhat in their two previous encounters but, when the sides met at Swansea in 1914, the French were "whacked" according to the *South Wales Daily News*. Superior in all phases, Wales chalked

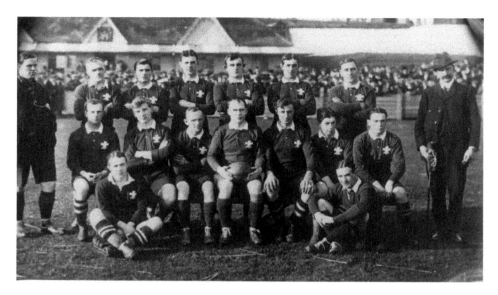

Wales v France 1914. Back: JB Jones, T Williams, E Morgan, TC Lloyd, D Watts, PL Jones; Middle: JJ Wetter, G Hirst, J Bancroft, Alban Davies, H Uzzell, JMC Lewis, WH Evans; Front: R Lloyd, IT Davies. [WRU]

up seven tries in an overwhelming victory by 31 points to 0. Lying in wait now were the Irish, some of whom were spoiling for a fight. With two wins and one loss, their record was as good as the Welshmen's. England had two games to complete yet, so, on paper at least, there was still everything to play for. Hoping to tip the balance in favour of the home team, one Irishman even offered each of the Welsh players ten pounds to throw the game!

Looking back over a lifetime in the sport in 1948, Townsend Collins declared, "rough games there have been in plenty: the roughest I ever saw was ... at Belfast in 1914." It seems that some of the Irish forwards, led by William Tyrrell, met up with their Welsh counterparts the night before the match and challenged them to a free-for-all the next day. This was eagerly accepted by Pontypool's Percy Jones on behalf of the Welsh and it set the character of the game.

Not all the players joined in the fighting which was largely, though not entirely, confined to the forwards. Dai was never specifically identified – few were – but it can be assumed that he was involved. The referee, for some reason, chose to ignore what went on. So too did many newspaper accounts, including those in *The Times* and the *Manchester Guardian* which made no reference to any fisticuffs. "Old Stager" rather played down the foul play, euphemistically commenting that the Irish forwards "had the surprise of their career in the dust ups started by Tyrrell, and were forced to acknowledge the strength, endurance, as well as the skill of their opponents." Mentioning no names, though the unidentified pugilists were almost certainly Jones and Tyrrell, "Old Stager" makes only one specific and rather dismissive comment about the fighting: "There was a dust up between a Welsh and an Irish forward but it did not call for official intervention." Yet Townsend Collins disagreed and wrote that many of the "fierce exchanges" took place off the ball, and enough happened under the very nose of the referee and in full view of the press box to justify sending off half-a-dozen culprits. "Scores of times men were tackled and flung to the ground when yards from the ball; frequently blows were exchanged; there were times when the game was more like a free fight than scientific Rugby football". But then he added somewhat ambivalently: "it was not malicious or bad-tempered. It was as if men had agreed to an hour's "all-in football" to find out who could take the most punishment. The Irishmen made the discovery about halfway through the second half."

The weather was atrocious. Pouring rain and a pitch which was a sea of mud were the kind of conditions with which many of the players would all too soon become familiar on the fields of France and Belgium. There was little open play. A heavy and greasy ball guaranteed the game would be dominated by the forwards. Ireland took the lead with a try but, with the Welsh backs on top and the pack eventually winning the battle up front, Wales hit back with three tries and a conversion to win by 11 points to 3. It was "a triumph not excelled for many seasons", thought the *Cardiff Times* and, had rather more care been taken in the selection for the England match, "the Triple Crown would have been secured." There was every reason to believe that Wales might be on the verge of a return to the glories of the previous decade.

The magnificent pack of 1914 remained unchanged all season, the first time this had ever happened. The *Manchester Guardian* gave them the highest praise. Not only were they the best eight by far in that year's Championship, but they were better than any of "the great Welsh packs of the past." According to "Old Stager", it was the former Irish international Joseph Magee who, during the match, turned to him and referred to them as "The Terrible Eight", a fitting battle honour which they have retained to the present day.

Even though Dai had just taken part in one of the most gruelling internationals of all time, there was no let up as he immediately returned to the challenging arena of the Glamorgan League. He grabbed a couple of tries in a vital 9-0 victory over Mountain Ash. This was followed by a 0-0 draw with Treorchy, in front of a record crowd – numbers no doubt boosted by his presence. Next up were Treherbert, though another 0-0 draw dashed Maesteg's

The Terrible Eight. Back: Percy Jones, Edgar Morgan, Harry Uzzell, TC Lloyd, Dai Watts; Front: Tom Williams, Alban Davies, Walter Rees (WRU Secretary), Jack "Bedwellty" Jones.

hopes of retaining the league title. Then there was a break from the regular grind with a holiday fixture against the touring Belfast Collegians, the 1913 Ulster league and cup champions. Here Dai became reacquainted with one of his recent opponents from the Irish match, though hostilities were not renewed because winger Jasper Brett had kept out of any of the fighting. He had played well against Wales and had a brilliant game against Maesteg, but was unable to prevent Collegians from going down by 8 points to 0. Jasper Brett is a sorry reminder that war can destroy minds as well as bodies. After fighting at Gallipoli and Salonika with the 7th (Service) Battalion The Royal Dublin Fusiliers, he was discharged from the Army with shell-shock in 1917 but took his life shortly afterwards.

Had there been a 1914-15 season, it is highly likely that Dai – now a proven international – would have been targeted by the senior clubs. There may be some evidence for this, for in April 1914 he "did a lot of good work" guesting for Bridgend in their 8-3 defeat at Swansea. Not that Bridgend were then a stronger club than Maesteg – they weren't – but this may be an indication that offers would have been made for him to move up to a higher grade of club rugby the following season. And, of course, there was always the likelihood that Northern Union agents would come calling, as they did for another Terrible Eight forward, Jack "Bedwellty" Jones, only a fortnight after the Belfast international.

But there never was another season for Dai. Instead of preparing for a further year in the Welsh jersey, he put on a uniform of a different kind after enlisting in Maesteg early in the war. Perhaps this was an unexpected opportunity to escape from the harshness of a life spent working underground. He joined the 7th (Service) Battalion The King's (Shropshire Light Infantry) which was formed at Shrewsbury in September 1914, but when Dai played in

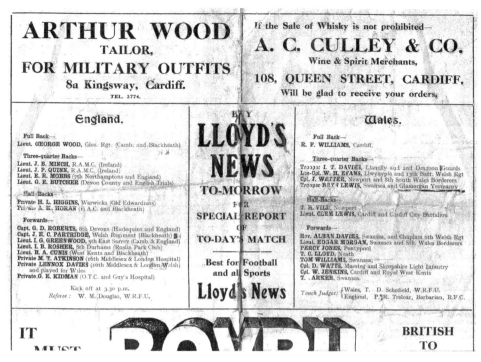

Wales v Barbarians ("England") match programme 1915.   [David Dow]

his last major game for an unofficial Welsh XV against the Barbarians at the Arms Park the following April, they had been in billets in Bournemouth for several months. By the time of this match, he had already been promoted to corporal. After final training at Aldershot, the 7th KSLI landed at Boulogne on 28 September 1915 and, within a few weeks of arriving in France, they were allocated to the 8th Brigade, 3rd Division.

Dai saw action in the Ypres Salient for some months before his battalion moved down to the Somme in July 1916. They arrived at the small village of Carnoy, just south of Mametz Wood, on the same day that the 16th Welsh were being slaughtered there in the first attack of the Welsh Division. The Shropshires, however, spent the following week preparing for their own blooding on the Somme, the Battle of Bazentin Ridge. They too were to suffer a fate similar to that of the ill-stared Cardiff City Battalion.

The British planned to assault the German line just north-east of Mametz Wood which had finally been captured on the 12 July after five days of bitter fighting. The plan was very different from that which had been devised for the catastrophic opening day of the Battle of the Somme two weeks earlier. It would take place at dawn using just four Divisions, allowing for a much greater concentration of supporting artillery fire. The troops would advance at night and lie up in no-man's-land to shorten the distance they would have to cover to get at the enemy. The artillery bombardment was to last just five minutes, which would be sufficient to drive the surviving Germans into their dugouts. Then the infantry would go in.

As Dai moved towards the KSLI's starting positions, he may have become aware, with some foreboding, of the aftermath of the Welsh Division's heroic endeavours at Mametz Wood. He probably did not know that amongst the casualties were two Welsh internationals and perhaps it was just as well that he didn't.

It is quite unlikely that many of the Shropshire lads had ever handled a rugby ball but it was to this sport that Dai turned as he tried to calm the nerves of the young men under his command just before the battle. According to Private George Isaacs:

> It was on the night of the 13th that we formed up for the attack; everyone knew there was hot work to be done but no-one seemed to trouble. It was as if the men were waiting to go for a football match or to the "pictures". Amid the roar of the guns one could hear Sgt. [sic] "Dai" Watts telling his platoon, "Now mind and heel the ball, boys: we've got a good three-quarter line ..." (meaning our guns). But this proved to be Dai's last match, poor chap – the last "international" in which he was able to help the old country to "score". His many friends will be consoled in knowing that he died, as a Britisher ought, doing his duty.

The KSLI reached their positions in no-man's-land by 11 p.m. There they spent a nerve-wracking wait of over four hours until, suddenly at 3.20 a.m. on 14 July, the guns roared into action and pounded the German line for exactly five minutes. Disastrously, some of the shells fell short and the Shropshires suffered their first casualties. The battalion's objectives were the enemy front trench and support line running through the remains of the village of Bazentin-le-Grand. At 3.25 a.m., as soon as the barrage lifted onto the German second line, the troops rose up and rushed towards their target. Elsewhere, the wire was destroyed and the attack largely successful but, as the 7th KSLI advanced, they found themselves confronted by two intimidating belts of wire ten to twenty yards thick. It was mostly untouched, the first belt barely cut and the second not at all.

Faced with this formidable obstacle, at first, none of the KSLI were able to get through. Caught at the wire, they became easy targets and many were cut down by machine-gun and rifle fire. The survivors of this onslaught were forced back to the shelter of a sunken road. Later they attacked again and, this time supported from the flank, they were able to cut through the wire and overrun the German trench and support line. Then they dug in to defend the newly-won position from several fierce German attacks until they were relieved several days later.

Despite their eventual success, it was a disastrous day for the 7th Shropshires who fared even worse than the 16th Welsh had a week earlier. They suffered an appalling 472 casualties, of whom 171 were fatalities, including Dai Watts, the last of the thirteen Welshmen to be capped. There appears to be no record of how Dai met his end. He may have been the victim of friendly artillery fire when waiting in no-man's-land. He may have been shot when desperately trying to get through the wire or he may have died leading his men into the German trenches.

Contemporary reports of his death refer to his having left a widow and two children. Like almost all of the 7th King's (Shropshire light Infantry) killed that day, Corporal David Watts has no known grave though, as we have seen, we can still pay tribute to the sacrifice of this fearless Welsh forward at the Thiepval Memorial to the Missing of the Somme. Not far from there, on 14 July 1916 during the Battle of Bazentin Ridge, the Terrible Eight were tragically reduced to seven.

Sergt. Dai Watts, K.S.L.I., killed. He was a well-known Maesteg international forward, and leaves a widow and two children.

Announcement of Dai's death in action.

Thiepval Memorial. [Gwyn Prescott]

Afterword

The Armistice had only been signed just two weeks earlier, but on 25 November 1918 the WRU resolved that all clubs were "now at liberty to arrange inter Club games." If rugby is anything, it is a life-affirming activity and players and officials quickly went about the business of getting the game going again. As the 1918-19 season wore on, more and more clubs began to appear in the results lists in the local press.

The international game began to revive too. Over the Christmas period, a Welsh XV played two matches against a New Zealand Military team. Field Marshall Haig even granted leave to several Welshmen to enable them to return home to play. Wales won the first match in Swansea and drew the second in Cardiff. These were unofficial matches, as were all games in 1918-19, apart from one. In April 1919, the WRU inconsistently sanctioned an *official* international at Swansea against the New Zealand Army team which had just triumphed in the King's Cup, a services international competition held throughout Britain. Only two previously capped players were selected for Wales, who this time went down to defeat by two penalty goals to one in a poor match. It probably didn't help that all fifteen had been involved in a game between a Welsh XV and the 38th (Welsh) Division only two days earlier. Since it was an official match, the WRU awarded caps to the Welsh players.

On the same day that the WRU gave its consent for clubs to play again, the Union resolved to dedicate a Roll of Honour of Welsh rugby players and consequently the secretary wrote to all clubs asking for a list of all those who had fallen in the war. The response, however, seems to have been disappointing. Maybe it was too soon for such a worthy initiative because, though establishing a reliable list of those who had not survived the war sounds simple enough, in practice it would have been no easy task for many clubs at this time. And this was on top of organising players, kit, fixtures, pitches and finances. Whatever the explanation, the matter seems to have been quietly dropped. As a result, sadly, the names of the vast majority of the many Welsh club players who died in the First World War are lost to the history of rugby.

This book has concentrated on the thirteen internationals who did not survive that war. But they were not the only casualties. There were some international players who died of wounds or whose deaths were hastened by their war experiences. One such was Hopkin Maddock, the record try scorer for London Welsh, who won six caps on the wing for Wales between 1906 and 1910. After enlisting in The Royal Fusiliers, "Hop" Maddock was commissioned in the Machine Gun Corps in 1916 and was awarded the Military Cross for his bravery in holding back the enemy near Peronne during the German Spring Offensive in March 1918. He was severely wounded in the shoulder and chest and eventually developed tuberculosis which led to his untimely death only three years after the war ended. Another Welsh international, who suffered greatly from his war injuries, was the magnificent forward David "Tarw" Jones. "Dai" was capped thirteen times and played in the victory over New Zealand before turning professional. He was seriously wounded while serving with the Welsh Guards and died aged fifty-one in 1933. Selwyn Biggs, who played nine times at half-back between 1895 and 1900, was badly gassed and was said to be an invalid for the rest of his life. These weren't the only ones. There were many who died before their time as a result of the dreadful privations they had suffered. And, in common with so many of that wonderful generation, all of whom have now sadly passed away, there were those "survivors" who had to carry the physical and mental scars of those awful years with them for the rest of their lives. They all deserve to be honoured.

Official rugby finally returned to Wales in 1919-20. Memories were still raw though when the Welsh team made their first post-war visit to Stade Colombes in February 1920. Players, officials and supporters solemnly gathered round a huge wreath, which was ceremoniously laid in front of the grandstand, and which bore the dedication:

> Lest we forget, 1920 – A tribute from the Welsh Rugby Union to players who fell in the war for freedom.

The day after the French match, which Wales won 6-5, the players and officials made a visit to the still-ravaged Somme battlefields. In following years, it became the practice for the Welsh team and officials to pay their respects at the Cenotaph on the Sunday after the Twickenham international.

We have seen that each of the thirteen internationals commemorated in this book contributed to a period of remarkable developments in the evolution of Welsh rugby; while those who played in the "First Golden Era" achieved a consistent level of success that would not be matched by Wales for another sixty years. This generation of players, therefore, should be remembered with honour and with pride.

Appendices

Appendix I: Maps *[Drawn by Terry Powell]*

Map 1: Armentières – Béthune – Loos

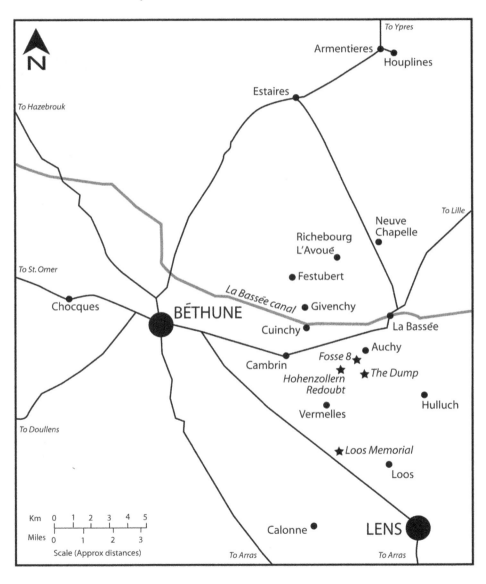

Map 2: Battle of Dogger Bank

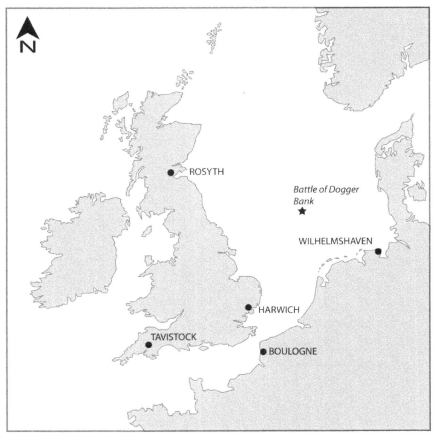

Map 3: Ypres Area

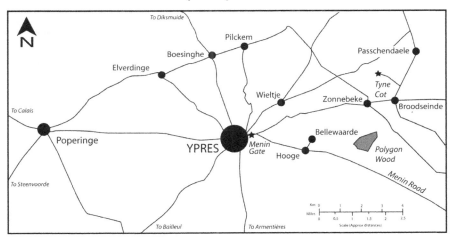

Map 4: The Somme

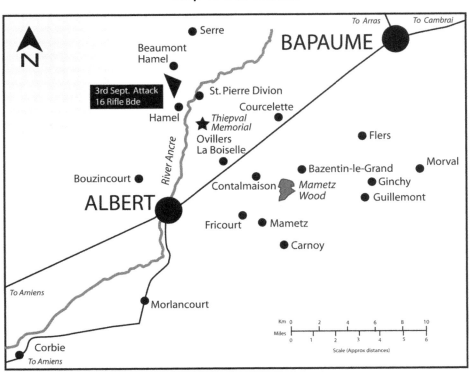

Map 5: Mametz Wood and Bazentin Ridge

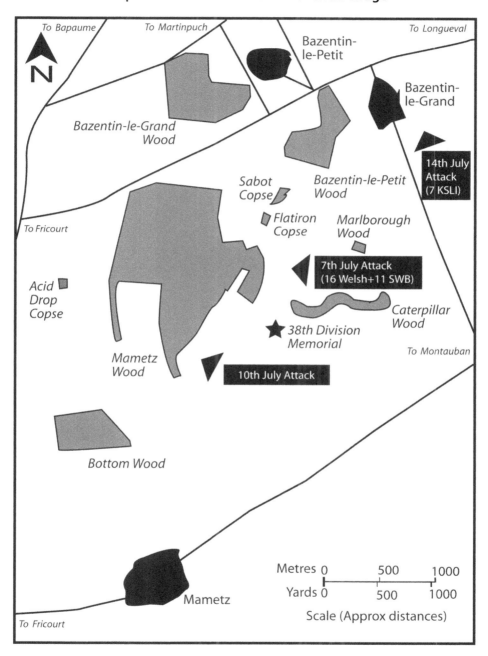

Map 6: Cambrai and Mormal Forest

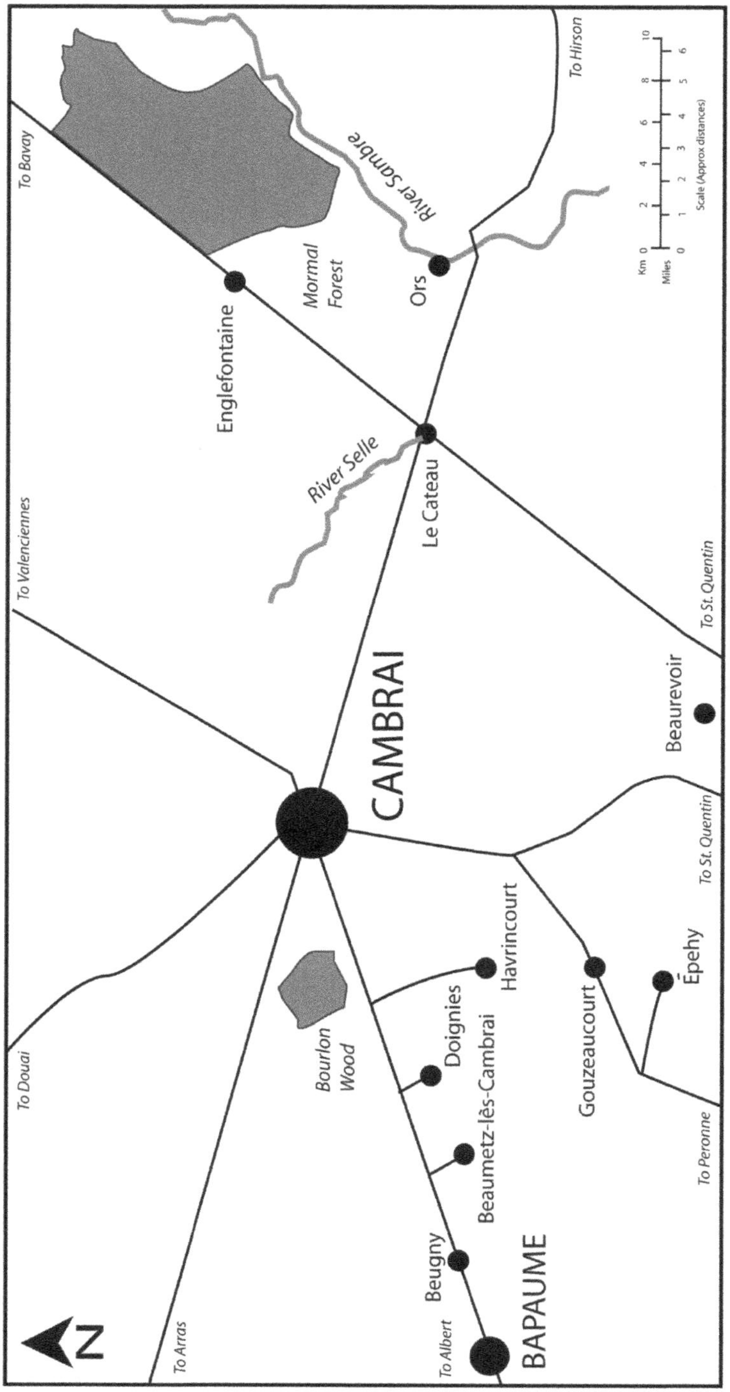

Appendix II: Rugby Internationals Roll of Honour

Argentina
FWC Sawyer

Australia
HW George
BD Hughes
HA Jones
ER Larkin
BI Swannell
WG Tasker
F Thompson
A Verge
CC Wallach

England
H Alexander
H Berry
AJ Dingle
GEB Dobbs
L Haigh
RHM Hands
AL Harrison
HA Hodges
RE Inglis
PD Kendal
JA King
RO Lagden
D Lambert
AF Maynard
ER Mobbs
WHB Nanson
FE Oakley
RL Pillman
RW Poulton
JE Raphael
RO Schwarz
LAN Slocock
FN Tarr
AF Todd

JHD Watson
AJ Wilson
CE Wilson

France
J Anduran
R Boudreaux
M Boyau
M Burgun
J Conihl de Beyssac
P Descamps
J Dufau
P Dupré
A Eutrope
M Giacardy
P Guillemin
M Hedembaigt
E Iguiniz
D Ihingoué
H Isaac
A Lacassagne
G Lane
L Larribau
M Legrain
A Mayssonnié
F Poeydebasque

Great Britain (Not otherwise capped)
CY Adamson
SN Crowther
RJ Rogers

Ireland
WJ Beatty
JT Brett
RB Burgess
EC Deane
WV Edwards
W Hallaran

B Maclear
GH McAllan
V McNamara
RS Smyth
AL Stewart
AS Taylor

New Zealand
JAS Baird
RS Black
H Dewar
EH Dodd
AJ Downing
D Gallaher
ET Harper
J McNeece
AJ Ridland
GMV Sellars
R Taylor
HS Turtill

Scotland
CH Abercrombie
DM Bain
DR Bedell-Sivright
PCB Blair
JA Campbell
WC Church
WM Dickson
WT Forrest
R Fraser
RE Gordon
JYM Henderson
DD Howie
JM Huggan
WR Hutchinson
GAW Lamond
E Milroy
TA Nelson

J Pearson
L Robertson
A Ross
J Ross
RF Simson
SSL Steyn
WR Sutherland
FH Turner
AL Wade
WM Wallace
JG Will
JS Wilson
ET Young

South Africa
AF Burdett
SA Ledger
TM Moll
JWH Morkel
G Thompson

USA
FJ Gard
RM Noble

Wales
WP Geen
BR Lewis
FL Perrett
LA Phillips
CM Pritchard
CG Taylor
HW Thomas
R Thomas
PD Waller
D Watts
D Westacott
JL Williams
RDG Williams

Further Reading

Rugby

Paul Beken and Stephen Jones, *Dragon in Exile: The Centenary History of London Welsh R.F.C.* (1985)

John Billott, *History of Welsh International Rugby* (1999)

Tony Collins, *A Social History of English Rugby Union* (2009)

W. J. Townsend Collins, *Rugby Recollections* (1948)

D. E. Davies, *Cardiff Rugby Club 1876-1975 History and Statistics: "The Greatest"* (1976)

Jack Davis, *One Hundred Years of Newport Rugby 1875-1975* (1974)

Alan Evans, *Taming the Tourists: How Cardiff Beat the All Blacks, Springboks and Wallabies* (2003)

Howard Evans, *Welsh International Matches 1881-2000* (1999)

David Farmer, *The Life and Times of Swansea R.F.C.: The All Whites* (1995)

Terry Godwin, *The Complete Who's Who of International Rugby* (1987)

Terry Godwin, *The International Rugby Championship 1883-1983* (1984)

John Griffiths, *The Phoenix Book of International Rugby Records* (1987)

John M. Jenkins, Duncan Pierce and Timothy Auty, *Who's Who of Welsh International Rugby Players* (1991)

Jennifer Macrory, *Running with the Ball: The Birth of Rugby Football* (1991)

Gwyn Prescott, *This Rugby Spellbound People: Rugby Football in Nineteenth-Century Cardiff and South Wales* (2011)

Huw Richards, *The Red and the White: The Story of England v Wales Rugby* (2009)

E. H. D. Sewell, *The Rugby Football Internationals' Roll of Honour* (1919)

David Smith and Gareth Williams, *Fields of Praise: The Official History of the Welsh Rugby Union 1881-1981* (1980)

Greg Thomas and Clem Thomas, *125 Years of the British and Irish Lions: The Official History* (2013)

Wayne Thomas, *A Century of Welsh Rugby Players 1880-1980* (1979)

Gareth Williams, *1905 and All That: Essays on Rugby Football, Sport and Welsh Society* (1991)

Military

Anon, *A History of the Seventy-First Siege Battery South African Heavy Artillery* (nd)

C. T. Atkinson, *The History of The South Wales Borderers, 1914-1918* (1931)

Reginald Berkeley, *The History of The Rifle Brigade in the War of 1914-1918, Volume I* (1927)

Sir Steuart Hare, *The Annals of The King's Royal Rifle Corps, Volume V, The Great War* (1932)

Colin Hughes, *Mametz – Lloyd George's 'Welsh Army' at the Battle of the Somme* (1990)

Richard Hough, *The Great War at Sea* (1983)

Thomas O. Marden, *The History of The Welch Regiment, Part II, 1914-1918* (1932)

Tony Mason and Eliza Riedi, *Sport and the Military: The British Armed Forces 1880-1960* (2010)

J. E. Munby (ed.), *A History of the 38th (Welsh) Division* (1920)

H. C. O'Neill, *The Royal Fusiliers in the Great War* (1922)

Andrew Rawson, *British Army Handbook 1914-1918* (2006)

Gary Sheffield, *Forgotten Victory – The First World War: Myths and Realities* (2002)

Julian Thompson, *The Imperial War Museum Book of the War at Sea 1914-1918 – The Face of Battle Revealed in the Words of the Men who Fought* (2005)

C. H. Dudley Ward, *History of The Welsh Guards* (1920)

C. H. Dudley Ward, *Regimental Records of The Royal Welch Fusiliers, Volume III, France and Flanders 1914-1918* (1928)

W. de B. Wood, *The History of The Kings Shropshire Light Infantry in the Great War* (1925)

Everard Wyrall, *The Gloucestershire Regiment in the War 1914-1918* (1931)

Websites

Commonwealth War Graves Commission: http://www.cwgc.org

The Long, Long Trail. The British Army in the Great War 1914-1918: http://www.1914-1918.net

The Western Front Association: http://www.westernfrontassociation.com

Wales Remembers 1914-1918: http://walesremembers.org